THE OXFORD BOOK OF
UPPER-VOICE POLYPHONY

A collection of sixteenth-century motets in two to six parts

EDITED BY **MARK KEANE**

MUSIC DEPARTMENT

OXFORD
UNIVERSITY PRESS

OXFORD
UNIVERSITY PRESS

Great Clarendon Street, Oxford OX2 6DP,
United Kingdom

Oxford University Press is a department of the University of Oxford.
It furthers the University's objective of excellence in research, scholarship,
and education by publishing worldwide. Oxford is a registered trade mark of
Oxford University Press in the UK and in certain other countries

This collection © Oxford University Press 2021

Mark Keane has asserted his right under the Copyright, Designs
and Patents Act, 1988, to be identified as the Editor of this Work

Database right Oxford University Press (maker)

First published 2021

Impression: 1

All rights reserved. No part of this publication may be reproduced,
stored in a retrieval system, or transmitted, in any form or by any means,
without the prior permission in writing of Oxford University Press

Permission to perform this work in public (except in the course of divine worship)
should normally be obtained from a local performing right licensing organization,
unless the owner or the occupier of the premises being used already holds
a licence from such an organization. Likewise, permission to make and
exploit a recording of these works should be obtained from a
local mechanical copyright licensing organization

Enquiries concerning reproduction outside the scope of the above
should be directed to the Music Rights Department, Oxford University Press,
at music.permissions.uk@oup.com or at the address above

ISBN 978-0-19-353485-8

Music and text origination by Katie Johnston
Printed in Great Britain on acid-free paper by
Halstan & Co. Ltd, Amersham, Bucks.

CONTENTS

1.	Agazzari	Magi videntes stellam	1
2.	Certon	Ave Maria	4
3.	Cifra	Ex ore infantium	7
4.	Clemens non Papa	Ego flos campi	10
5.	Cristo	Audi Israel	13
6.	Cristo	Dum complerentur dies Pentecostes	19
7.	Cristo	Princeps gloriosissime	25
8.	d'Este	Sicut lilium inter spinas	30
9.	Gombert	Quam pulchra es	34
10.	Guerrero	Sancta et immaculata virginitas	43
11.	Handl	Ante luciferum genitus	50
12.	Handl	Haec est dies	54
13.	Handl	O beata Trinitas	60
14.	Handl	O sacrum convivium	65
15.	Ingegneri	Estote fortes in bello	71
16.	Josquin des Prez	Alma Redemptoris Mater	76
17.	Lassus	Adoramus te, Christe (a 5)	87
18.	Lassus	Adoramus te, Christe (a 3)	90
19.	Lassus	Agimus tibi gratias	92
20.	Lassus	In pace in idipsum dormiam	94
21.	Lassus	Justus cor suum tradet	96
22.	Lassus	Oculus non vidit	98
23.	Massaino	Cum pervenisset beatus Andreas	100
24.	Massaino	Surge, propera, amica mea	107
25.	Merulo	Dum illucescente	117
26.	Merulo	Jubilate Deo	121
27.	Monteverdi	Ave Maria	124
28.	Monteverdi	Lauda Sion	126
29.	Monteverdi	O Domine Jesu Christe	128
30.	Morales	O magnum mysterium	131
31.	Morales	Regina caeli	136
32.	Palestrina	Alma Redemptoris Mater	142
33.	Palestrina	Confitemini Domino	151
34.	Palestrina	Jesu, Rex admirabilis	155
35.	Palestrina	Pueri Hebraeorum	156
36.	Sheppard	Magnificat	161
37.	Taverner	Audivi vocem de caelo	178
38.	Victoria	Duo Seraphim	183
39.	Victoria	Judas mercator pessimus	191
40.	Victoria	O Regem caeli	195
41.	Victoria	O sacrum convivium	207
42.	Victoria	O vos omnes	214
43.	Victoria	Tenebrae factae sunt	217

Commentary   221

PREFACE

The Oxford Book of Upper-Voice Polyphony provides equal-voice choirs with an extensive collection of polyphony hitherto only available as individual titles or as part of smaller collections, some of which is printed here for the first time in modern notation. The selection of compositions included in this anthology is a personal choice of the editor and comprises Latin polyphonic compositions exclusively. It is an excellent resource with which to introduce upper-voice choirs to this repertoire and contains motets that can be used throughout the liturgical year, with scoring from two parts through to double chorus. While a large canon of music exists for upper-voice choirs accompanied by continuo and bass viol, or other consort wind instruments, the fundamental focus of this publication is to present a collection of music for *a cappella* performance in the classroom, concert hall, or church. The pieces contained in the anthology offer a *coup d'œil* into the vast range of equal-voice compositions from the so-called 'golden era' of choral composition, which has been eclipsed by the more well-known mixed-voice repertoire.

The sources for equal-voice compositions are often labelled as *voci pari* (or *voces pares*, *voix pareilles*, *voces ad aequales*, *voces mutatae*). This scoring may have been chosen by a composer in response to their available vocal resources, such as for choirs in a monastery or convent, or for boys' voices only. Other plausible reasons for the scoring include a deliberate intention by the composer to increase expressivity in the chosen text, or a commercial strategy on the part of publishers to exploit a niche market. It was common to find a small number of *voci pari* compositions in mixed-voice (*voci pieni*) publications from the era. Examples include Victoria's *O Regem caeli*, which was printed in a 1572 collection that is predominantly for mixed voices, and similarly Guerrero's *Sancta et immaculata virginitas*, which appeared in a 1589 mixed-voice publication. It is interesting to note that printers often retained the traditional CATB labelling (cantus, altus, tenor, bassus—similar to the modern SATB choral scoring) when publishing *voci pari* partbooks, possibly owing to the existence of ready-made title woodblocks for printing. The most important aspect in identifying *voci pari* scoring is therefore the choice of clefs, rather than the vocal labelling. For treble voices, this typically comprised a combination of high clefs, which include treble clefs (G_2 clefs) and alto clefs (C_3 clefs) and is known as *chiavi alte* or *chiavette*. The exact clef combinations differ from composer to composer and even from piece to piece.

A practice of fluidity between the scoring of high clefs (for treble voices) and low clefs (for male voices) in *voci pari* composition is witnessed in publications in the 1540s. When Cristóbal de Morales's setting of *Candida virginitas* was published by Girolamo Scotto in 1543, it used the high-clef combination G_2–G_2–C_1–C_3, but when it was reprinted six years later by Antonio Gardano, the piece employed the low-clef combination C_3–C_4–C_4–F_4, sounding an octave lower than the first edition and indicating performance by *voces mutatae*, or mature male voices. Another example is the anonymous five-voice setting of *O salutaris hostia* from 1543, which used the high-clef combination G_2–G_2–C_1–C_1–C_3, whereas the reprint in 1549 used the low-clef combination C_3–C_4–C_4–F_3–F_4. These examples establish a precedence for *voci pari* compositions moving liberally between upper-voice and lower-voice ensembles. With this in mind, some motets in this anthology, including those by Gombert, Handl, Josquin, and Sheppard, originally scored with low clefs, have been transposed up an octave for upper-voice choirs. This practice of alternative vocal options for male and female voices, disregarding the clefs presented in collections, continued into the seventeenth century, including a publication by Johann Donfrid in 1622, which provides optional voicing for a significant number of motets in the index.[1] In this collection, motets originally conceived for treble voices have also been transposed, in some cases, to suit modern upper-voice ranges.

The use of high clefs has accumulated much analysis by musicologists, including Andrew Parrott, Patrizio Barbieri, and Andrew Johnstone.[2] Each one has suggested various options for transposing music printed with high clefs down by an interval of between a second and a fifth for performance by a

---

[1] Johann Donfrid, *Promptuarii musici concentus ecclesiasticos* (Strasbourg, 1622).
[2] Andrew Parrott, 'Transposition in Monteverdi's Vespers of 1610: An "aberration" defended', *Early Music*, 12 (1984), 490–516; Andrew Parrott, 'Monteverdi: Onwards and downwards', *Early Music*, 32 (2004), 303–17; Patrizio Barbieri, '"Chiavette" and modal transposition in Italian practice (c.1500–1837)', *Recercare*, 3 (1991), 5–79; Andrew Johnstone, '"High" clefs in composition and performance', *Early Music*, 34 (2006), 29–53.

Preface

mixed-voice choir rather than equal voices. However, where a printed edition includes the text *voci pari*, such transpositions, while possible, are clearly not the intention of the composer. While there is ample empirical evidence from sixteenth-century theorists and composers alike of this downward transposition for mixed voices,[3] for each example there are other sources supporting the fact that compositions notated in high clefs should not be transposed.[4] One of the most unique pieces in this collection is Tiburzio Massaino's *Cum pervenisset beatus Andreas*, which was printed with five G_2 clefs, meaning no transposition for mixed voices is possible.

Scholarly research by Craig Monson, Robert Kendrick, and Laurie Stras, which has explored Italian convent music in the sixteenth and seventeenth centuries, has greatly influenced the contents of this anthology.[5] The setting of *Sicut lilium inter spinas* from the anonymous 1543 publication, *Musica quinque vocum: motetta materna lingua vocata*, is of particular interest.[6] Stras has attributed the authorship of this collection to the nun and composer Leonora d'Este (1515–75), and has developed a strong case, which is examined in greater detail in the commentary.[7] Cornerstones of the *voci pari* tradition by Palestrina, Lassus, and Victoria have been included alongside works by other composers who may not be as familiar to contemporary audiences. The aim of the anthology is to provide a solid foundation for upper-voice choirs wanting to explore this broad and beautiful music, from which they can expand their repertoire to perform other motets originally conceived for this vocal ensemble.

Editorial practice

The Oxford Book of Upper-Voice Polyphony has been compiled and edited using primary sources exclusively. The sources are referenced in the commentary with *Grove* library sigla, followed by the title, place, and year of publication, where known. The aim has been to keep each score as uncluttered as possible to assist choirs in their reading and interpretation of the music.

A significant number of the pieces in this anthology were transcribed from one extant source, which precludes the development of a critical edition, cross-referencing, and comparative analysis. The variants included in the commentary are deliberately few to avoid repetition of material in the notation on the scores and the accompanying text. Prefatory staves provided at the beginning of each piece illustrate the original clefs, time signature, key signature, and the first pitch note and value in square notation, as well as the name of the original partbook or voice, where given. Editorial accidentals appear above the vocal line in small type. All note values have been reduced to give a ♩ pulse, but in performance practice, conductors offering two ♩ beats in a bar will achieve a more stylized result from choirs performing this repertoire. The ♩ beat also facilitates smoother transitions between the rhythmic-related duple and triple metre sections. The choice of key signature and transposition is a personal perspective of the editor to suit standard upper-voice ranges and these are noted in the commentary.

The Latin texts follow modernized conventions relating to spelling, capitalization, and punctuation, and both the *Liber Usualis* and *The Oxford Latin Dictionary* were consulted to establish a consistent approach. Some words such as *caeli*, which has multiple spelling variations in the sources (*e.g. coeli, celi*), have been standardized. Editorially completed text underlay is not shown in italics, and indications of ligatures and coloration have been removed in order to present an uncluttered score. The sources have often been unclear with regard to syllable allocation. Different prints and editions have been consulted, but where this was not possible a stylistic approach of adhering to the accents in spoken text has been taken. The translations printed at the foot of each score are non-literal and should assist

---

[3] Adriano Banchieri, *Cartella Musicale* (Venice, 1601) and *Ecclesiastiche Sinfonie* (Venice, 1607); Giovanni Francesco Anerio, *Antiphonae, seu sacrae cantiones* (Rome, 1613); Lodovico Viadana, *Cento concerti ecclesiastici* (Venice, 1602).

[4] Girolamo Frescobaldi, *Il Primo Libro delle Canzoni* (Rome, 1628); Claudio Monteverdi, *Madrigali guerrieri et amorosi* (Venice, 1638).

[5] Craig Monson, *Divas in the Convent: Nuns, Music, and Defiance in Seventeenth-Century Italy* (Chicago: The University of Chicago Press, 2012) and *Disembodied Voices: Music and Culture in an Early Modern Italian Convent* (California: University of California Press, 1995); Robert Kendrick, *Celestial Sirens: Nuns and their Music in Early Modern Milan* (Oxford: Clarendon Press, 1996); Laurie Stras, *Women and Music in Sixteenth-Century Ferrara* (Cambridge: Cambridge University Press, 2018).

[6] Anon., *Musica quinque vocum: motetta materna lingua vocata* (Venice, 1543).

[7] Laurie Stras, *Women and Music in Sixteenth-Century Ferrara* (Cambridge: Cambridge University Press, 2018).

choirs in their overall interpretation of the motet. The editorial decision to omit an option of singing the pieces in English was taken in the initial development of the collection, primarily to be faithful to the Latin tradition, and also to avoid translations that would be less effective with the music, phrasing, or accents.

Keyboard reductions are provided for rehearsal use only and are presented in their most readable and playable form using two treble clefs throughout. Owing to the continuous overlapping of vocal lines, the movement between individual parts could not be replicated in the reductions. The consequence is a presentation of parallel octaves and fifths, but this was considered more beneficial than the untidy crossing of upstems and downstems. In tendering uncluttered reductions, *musica ficta* have been incorporated without qualification to avoid incessant use of small and bracketed accidentals in and above the score. Accidentals follow the standard convention of homophonic keyboard music and are not duplicated within a bar. Keyboard reductions have been deemed unnecessary for the two-part and three-part compositions.

The tempo and dynamic indications are editorial; while some conductors will find them irritating, to others they provide a starting point in their exploration of the repertoire. The most important aspect in the practice of singing polyphony is the shaping and phrasing of each line, and subsequently how these weave together to create a complex texture and an aural plurality of layers. Editorial hairpins have been kept to a minimum to enable conductors and singers to consider the shape of each phrase. The most successful performances achieve a heterogeneous soundscape in their layering, noting the rise and fall of dynamics, accents, and stresses to mirror the spoken text, and consistent shaping within each individual phrase.

Acknowledgements

I wish to express my sincere thanks to the many people who have assisted me in my research for this anthology for upper voices. I would like to recognize, in particular, the staff from libraries where the primary sources were gathered, especially Marta Crippa, Biblioteca del Conservatorio di Musica 'Giuseppe Verdi', Milan; Fra Carlo Bottero, Biblioteca del Sacro Convento di San Francesco, Assisi; Àngels Rius i Bou, Biblioteca de l'Abadia de Montserrat; and Fausto Roldán, Biblioteca Bartolomé March, Palma de Mallorca; as well as the staff at the Archivo de la Catedral de Toledo; Archivo Ducal de Medinaceli; Biblioteca Geral da Universidade de Coimbra; Rare Books and Music department of the British Library; Bayerische Staatsbibliothek, Munich; Thüringer Universitäts und Landesbibliothek, Jena; Santini-Bibliothek, Münster; Bibliothèque Royale de Belgique, Brussels; and University of Pennsylvania Libraries, Philadelphia. I am very grateful to Anthony Pryer for allowing me to consult his edition of Monteverdi's *Sacrae cantiunculae*, and to Michael Noone for his correspondence about the sources relating to the works of Morales.

I especially want to thank Robyn Elton, Commissioning Editor in Music at Oxford University Press, as well as editors Laura Jones and Anna Williams, for providing invaluable support and advice throughout the editing process leading to publication. I am also greatly indebted to my many friends and colleagues who offered to proofread different sections from the book. I wish to dedicate *The Oxford Book of Upper-Voice Polyphony* in memory of Mary Dale, who was my first organ tutor and introduced me to the art of singing polyphony in Galway Cathedral. It is my greatest wish that this book will assist, inspire, and expand the choral tradition of Renaissance polyphony for generations to come.

MARK KEANE
May 2020

1. Magi videntes stellam

Antiphon for the Feast of the Epiphany
(Matthew 2: 1–2)

AGOSTINO AGAZZARI
(c.1580–1642)

Translation:
The Magi, seeing the star, said to each other:
This is the sign of a great king.
Let us go and look for him and offer him gifts,
Gold, frankincense, and myrrh. Alleluia.

Duration: 2 mins

© Oxford University Press 2021. Photocopying this copyright material is ILLEGAL.

2 Agazzari: Magi videntes stellam

33
[p]
[mf]
[f]
myr - rham, au - rum, thus et myr - rham, au - rum, thus et myr - rham. Al-le-
[p]
[mf]
myr - rham, au - rum, thus et myr - rham, au - rum, thus et myr - rham.
[f]
myr - rham, au - rum, thus et myr - rham. Al-le-
38
-lu-ia, al-le-lu - ia, al-le-lu-ia, al-le - lu - ia, al-le - lu-ia, al-le-lu-ia, al - le-
[f]
Al-le-lu-ia, al-le - lu - ia, al-le - lu-ia, al-le-lu - ia, al-le-lu-ia, al-le -
-lu-ia, al-le - lu-ia, al-le-lu - ia, al-le-lu-ia, al-le - lu-ia, al-le-lu-ia, al-le -
42
[p]
[mf]
- lu - ia, al-le - lu-ia, al-le-lu - ia, al-le-lu-ia, al-le - lu - ia, al-le-
[p]
[mf]
- lu - ia, al-le-lu-ia, al-le - lu - ia, al-le - lu-ia, al-le-lu - ia,
[p]
[mf]
- lu - ia, al-le - lu-ia, al-le - lu-ia, al-le-lu - ia, al-le-lu-ia, al-le-
46
[f]
-lu - ia, al - le - lu - ia, al - le - lu - ia, al - le - lu-ia, al - le - lu - ia.
[f]
al - le - lu - ia, al - le - lu - ia, al - le - lu - ia, al - le - lu - ia.
[f]
-lu - ia, al - le - lu - ia, al - le - lu - ia, al - le - lu - ia, al - le - lu - ia.

2. Ave Maria

The Angelic Salutation

PIERRE CERTON
(d. 1572)

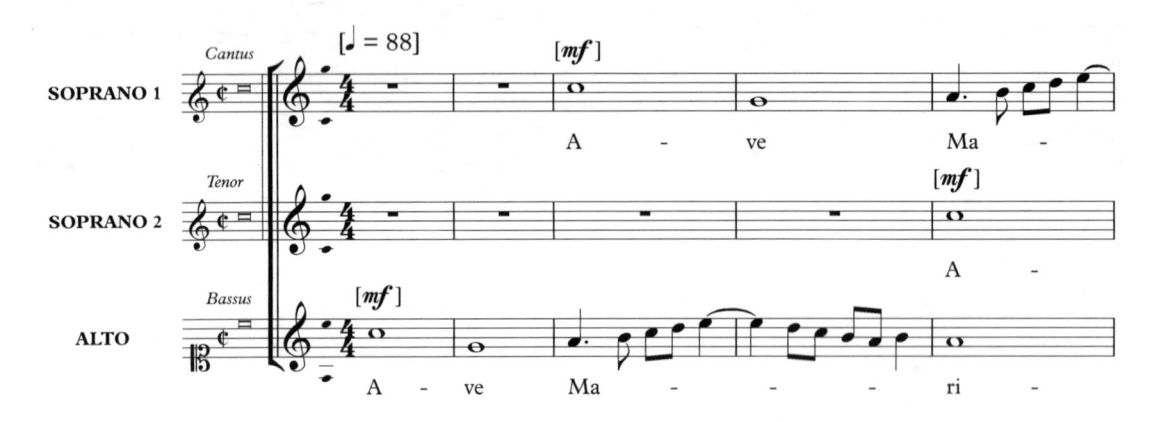

Duration: 2 mins

Translation:
Hail Mary, full of grace, the Lord is with thee,
Blessed art thou among women.

© Oxford University Press 2021. Photocopying this copyright material is ILLEGAL.

Certon: Ave Maria 5

6 Certon: Ave Maria

3. Ex ore infantium

Introit for the Feast of the Holy Innocents
Psalm 8: 3 (2)

ANTONIO CIFRA
(1584–1629)

Translation:
From the mouths of children and infants you have perfected praise,
Because of your enemies, that you may destroy the enemy and the avenger.

Duration: 1 min

© Oxford University Press 2021. Photocopying this copyright material is ILLEGAL.

8 Cifra: Ex ore infantium

Cifra: Ex ore infantium

4. Ego flos campi

Song of Songs 2: 1–3

JACOBUS CLEMENS non PAPA
(c.1510–1555/6)

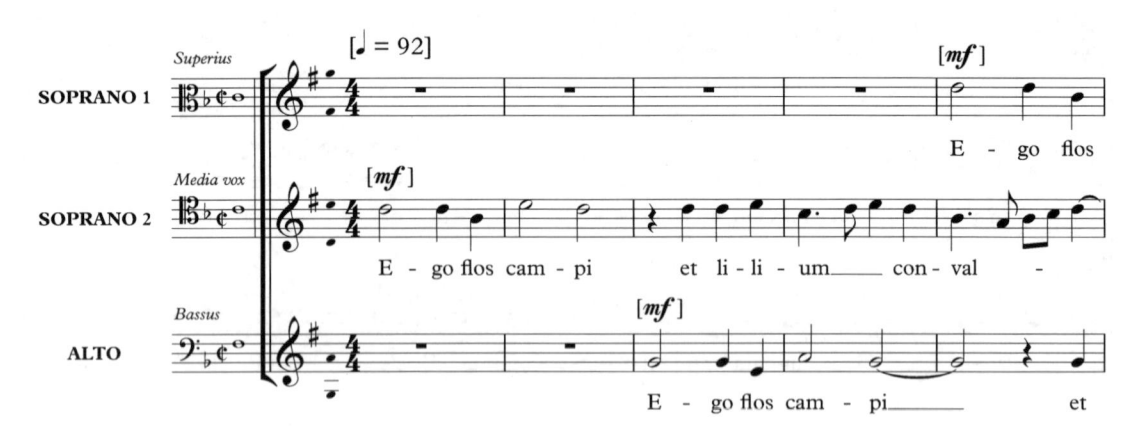

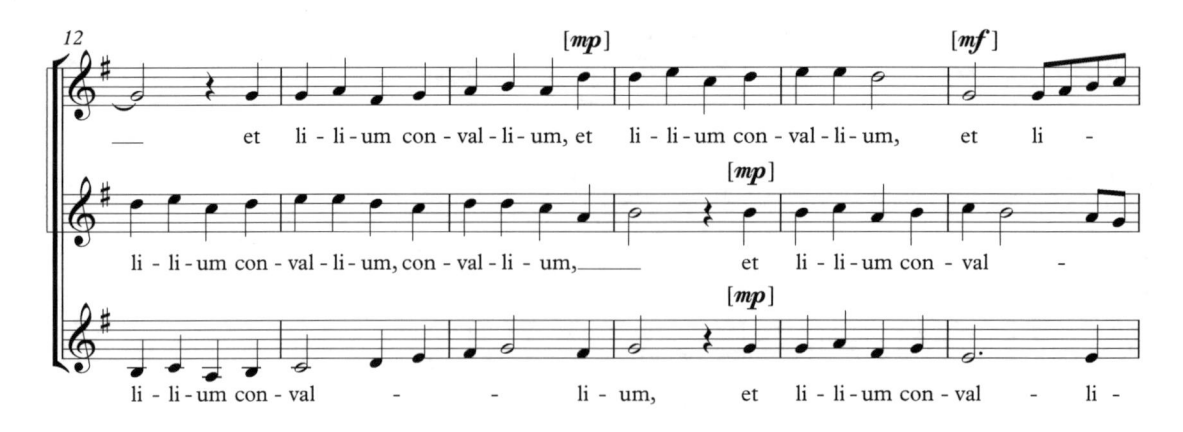

Duration: 2.5 mins

Translation:
I am the rose of the field and the lily of the valleys.
As the lily is among the thorns, so is my love among the daughters.
As the apple tree among the trees of the wood, so is my beloved among the sons.

© Oxford University Press 2021. Photocopying this copyright material is ILLEGAL.

18
- li - um con-val - li - um. Si - cut li - li -
[mf]
- li - um. Si - cut li - li-um in - ter spi-nas, in - ter spi-
[mf]
-um, con - val-li - um. Si - cut li - li - um in - ter spi -
24
-um in-ter spi - nas, spi - - nas, si - cut
- nas, in - ter spi-nas, si - cut
- - nas, si - cut li - li-um in - ter spi -
29
li - li - um in - ter spi - - - nas,
[mp]
li - li - um in - ter spi - - - nas, sic a - mi-ca me-a
[mp]
- - nas, in - ter spi - nas, sic a - mi-ca
34
[mp]
sic a - mi-ca me-a in - ter fi - li-as, sic
in - ter fi - li - as, fi - - li - as, sic a - mi - ca me-a
me-a in-ter fi - li - as, sic a-mi - ca me-a in-ter

12 Clemens non Papa: Ego flos campi

5. Audi Israel

Responsory for the Fourth Sunday of Lent
(Exodus 23: 22; Deuteronomy 6: 3 and 27: 3)

PEDRO de CRISTO
(*c.*1550–1618)

Duration: 2.5 mins

Translation:
Listen, Israel, to the rules of the Lord, in your heart as it is written in a book,
And I will give you a land flowing with milk and honey.
Observe and listen to me,
And I will be an enemy to your enemies.

© Oxford University Press 2021. Photocopying this copyright material is ILLEGAL.

14 Cristo: Audi Israel

Cristo: Audi Israel **15**

16 Cristo: Audi Israel

Cristo: Audi Israel **17**

18 Cristo: Audi Israel

6. Dum complerentur dies Pentecostes

Antiphon for the Feast of Pentecost
Acts 2: 1–2

PEDRO de CRISTO
(c.1550–1618)

Translation:
When the day of Pentecost had come, the disciples were all together in one place,
And suddenly there came a sound from heaven,
Like the blowing of a violent wind,
And it filled the whole house where they were sitting. Alleluia.

© Oxford University Press 2021. Photocopying this copyright material is ILLEGAL.

20 Cristo: Dum complerentur dies Pentecostes

Cristo: Dum complerentur dies Pentecostes 21

22 Cristo: Dum complerentur dies Pentecostes

Cristo: Dum complerentur dies Pentecostes 23

24 Cristo: Dum complerentur dies Pentecostes

7. Princeps gloriosissime

Antiphon at Michaelmas

PEDRO de CRISTO
(*c*.1550–1618)

Translation:
O most glorious Prince, Michael the Archangel, be mindful of us;
Here and everywhere, always pray for us to the Son of God. Alleluia.

Duration: 2 mins

© Oxford University Press 2021. Photocopying this copyright material is ILLEGAL.

26 Cristo: Princeps gloriosissime

Cristo: Princeps gloriosissime **27**

28 Cristo: Princeps gloriosissime

Cristo: Princeps gloriosissime **29**

8. Sicut lilium inter spinas

Antiphon for the Feast of the Assumption of the BVM
Song of Songs 2: 2

anon. attrib. LEONORA d'ESTE
(1515–75)

Translation:
As the lily is among the thorns, so is my love among the daughters.

© Oxford University Press 2021. Photocopying this copyright material is ILLEGAL.

d'Este: Sicut lilium inter spinas **31**

32 d'Este: Sicut lilium inter spinas

d'Este: Sicut lilium inter spinas

9. Quam pulchra es

Song of Songs 7: 4–12 (adap.)

NICOLAS GOMBERT
(c.1495–c.1560)

Duration: 5 mins

Translation:
How beautiful and fair you are,
My beloved, most sweet in your delights.
Your stature is like a palm-tree
And your breasts are like fruit.
Your head is like Mount Carmel
And your neck an ivory tower.
Come, my beloved, let us go into the fields,
And see if the blossoms have borne fruit,
And if the pomegranates have flowered.
There I will give you my love.

© Oxford University Press 2021. Photocopying this copyright material is ILLEGAL.

Gombert: Quam pulchra es

36 Gombert: Quam pulchra es

Gombert: Quam pulchra es

38 Gombert: Quam pulchra es

66
e-burn-ne - - a. Ve - ni di - le - cte mi, ve - ni di-
- - - - - - a. Ve - ni di-le-cte mi, ve - ni
tur-ris e - bur - ne - - - - a. Ve-ni di-le - cte mi,
- bur - ne - a. Ve - ni di - le-cte mi, ve - ni di - le-cte mi,
f
73
-le - cte mi, ve-ni di-le - - - cte mi, e - gre-di - a-mur
di - le-cte mi, ve - ni di - le - cte mi, e - gre-di - a-mur in a -
ve - ni di - le - - cte mi, e - gre-di - a-mur in a-grum no-
ve - ni di-le-cte mi, ve - ni di-le - cte mi,
mp

40 Gombert: Quam pulchra es

93
- runt ma-la pu - ni - ca, ma - la pu - -
-ru - e - runt ma - la pu - ni - ca, ma - la pu - - ni - ca.
-ru - e - runt ma - la pu - - - -
pu-ni-ca, ma-la pu - ni - ca, ma - la pu - -
mp mf

100
- ni - ca. Ti - bi da-bo u - be-ra me - -
Ti - bi da - bo u - be - - ra me - - - a, ti - bi da - bo
- ni - ca. Ti - bi da - bo u - be - ra me - - - a, u-
- ni - ca. Ti - bi da - bo u - be - ra me - a, ti - bi da-bo u-
mp mf

42 Gombert: Quam pulchra es

10. Sancta et immaculata virginitas

Responsory at Matins for Christmas
Feast days of the BVM

FRANCISCO GUERRERO
(1528–99)

Duration: 3.5 mins

Translation:
O holy and immaculate virginity,
I know not by what praises I may extol thee:
For thou hast borne in thy womb
He whom the heavens could not contain.
Blessed art thou among women,
And blessed is the fruit of thy womb.

© Oxford University Press 2021. Photocopying this copyright material is ILLEGAL.

44 Guerrero: Sancta et immaculata virginitas

Guerrero: Sancta et immaculata virginitas

46 Guerrero: Sancta et immaculata virginitas

53
-di - cta tu in mu - li - e - ri - bus, in mu - li - e - ri - bus,
be - ne - di - cta tu in mu - li - e - ri - bus, in mu - li - e - ri - bus,
in mu - li - e - ri - bus, in mu - li - e - ri - bus, et be - ne -
-e - ri - bus, in mu - li - e - ri - bus, in mu - li - e - ri - bus,
mp mf
59
et be - ne - di - ctus fru - ctus ven - tris tu - i, fru -
et be - ne - di - ctus fru - ctus ven - tris tu -
-di - ctus fru - ctus ven - tris tu - i, fru - ctus ven - tris tu -
et be - ne - di - ctus fru - ctus ven - tris tu - i, fru - ctus ven -

48 Guerrero: Sancta et immaculata virginitas

Guerrero: Sancta et immaculata virginitas

11. Ante luciferum genitus

Antiphon for the Feast of the Epiphany

JACOBUS HANDL
(1550–91)

Duration: 1.5 mins

Translation:
Born before the day star
And before the ages,
The Lord our Saviour has appeared to the world today. Alleluia.

© Oxford University Press 2021. Photocopying this copyright material is ILLEGAL.

Handl: Ante luciferum genitus **51**

52 Handl: Ante luciferum genitus

Handl: Ante luciferum genitus 53

12. Haec est dies

Gradual Easter Sunday
Psalm 117 (118): 24

JACOBUS HANDL
(1550–91)

** Original clefs for first sopranos and altos shown here. Choir 1 second soprano (*Altus*) and Choir 2 second soprano (*Septima*) were written: — Choir 1 second alto (*Bassus*) and Choir 2 second alto (*Octava*) were written:*

Duration: 2.5 mins

Translation:
This is the day that the Lord has made: let us rejoice and be glad in it. Alleluia.

© Oxford University Press 2021. Photocopying this copyright material is ILLEGAL.

Handl: Haec est dies 55

56 Handl: Haec est dies

Handl: Haec est dies

al - le - lu - ia, al - le - lu - ia, al - le - lu - ia,

-ia, al - le - lu - ia, al - le - lu - ia, al - le - lu -

ex - sul - te - mus et lae - te - mur in e - a,

-ia,

58 Handl: Haec est dies

Handl: Haec est dies

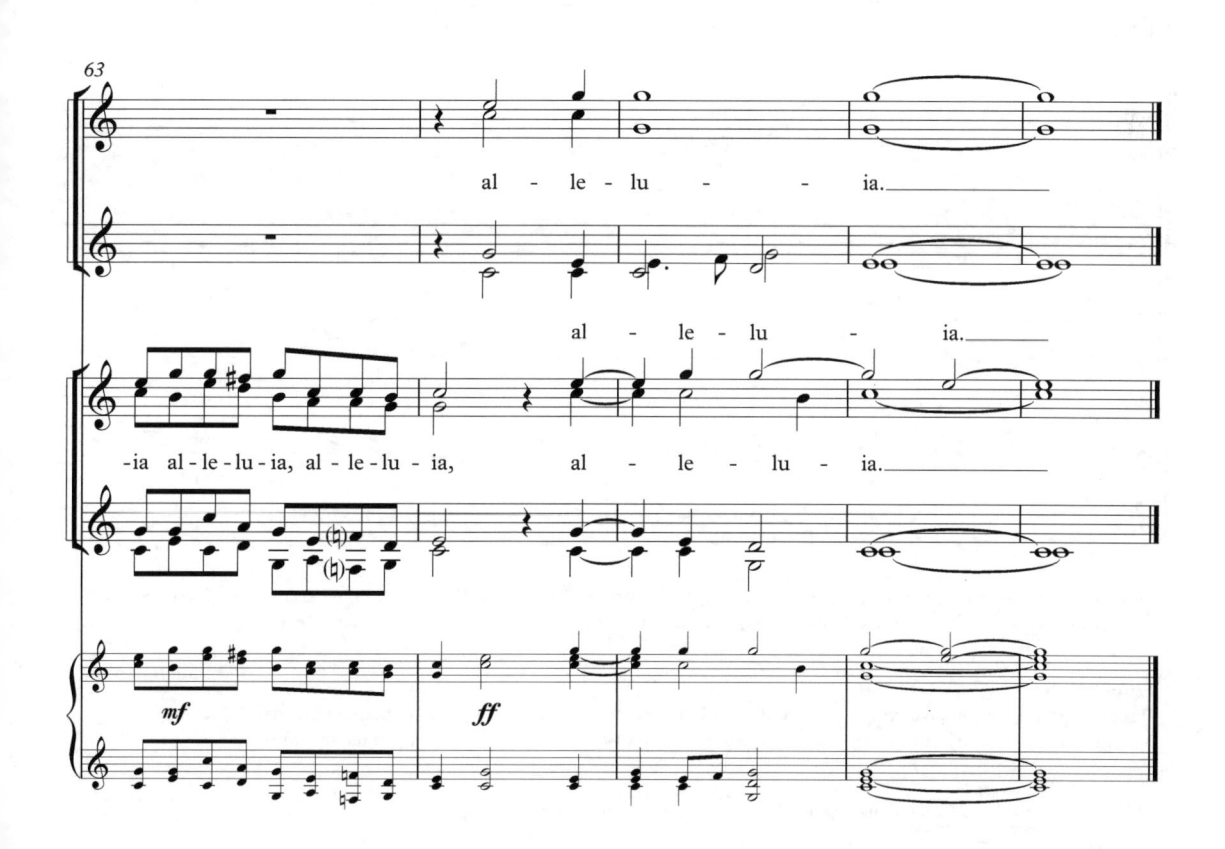

13. O beata Trinitas

Feast of the Holy Trinity

JACOBUS HANDL
(1550–91)

* Original clefs for first sopranos and altos shown here. Choir 1 second soprano (*Altus*) and Choir 2 second soprano (*Septima*) were written: 𝄡 Choir 1 second alto (*Bassus*) and Choir 2 second alto (*Octava*) were written: 𝄢

Duration: 2 mins

Translation:
O blessed Trinity, we invoke you,
We praise you, we adore you.

O blessed Trinity, our hope,
Our safety, our glory.

O blessed Trinity, deliver us,
Save us, live in us.

© Oxford University Press 2021. Photocopying this copyright material is ILLEGAL.

Handl: O beata Trinitas

62 Handl: O beata Trinitas

34
li - be - ra nos, sal - va
be - a - ta Tri - ni - tas, li - be - ra nos,
p
mp
39
nos, vi - vi - fi - ca nos, li - be - ra nos, sal - va nos,
sal - va nos, vi - vi - fi - ca nos,
mf
p
mp

64 Handl: O beata Trinitas

14. O sacrum convivium

Antiphon for the Feast of Corpus Christi

JACOBUS HANDL
(1550–91)

Duration: 3 mins

Translation:
O sacred banquet, in which Christ is received,
The memory of his Passion is recalled,
The mind is filled with grace,
And a pledge of future glory is given to us. Alleluia.

© Oxford University Press 2021. Photocopying this copyright material is ILLEGAL.

66 Handl: O sacrum convivium

Handl: O sacrum convivium

68 Handl: O sacrum convivium

Handl: O sacrum convivium

70 Handl: O sacrum convivium

15. Estote fortes in bello

Feast of the Apostles and Evangelists

MARC' ANTONIO INGEGNERI
(1535/6–92)

Translation:
Be valiant in war,
And fight the ancient serpent,
And you will receive the everlasting kingdom. Alleluia.

© Oxford University Press 2021. Photocopying this copyright material is ILLEGAL.

Duration: 2 mins

72 Ingegneri: Estote fortes in bello

Ingegneri: Estote fortes in bello 73

74 Ingegneri: Estote fortes in bello

Ingegneri: Estote fortes in bello

16. Alma Redemptoris Mater

Marian Antiphon
attrib. Hermann of Reichenau (1013–54)

JOSQUIN des PREZ
(c.1450–1521)

Duration: 4.5 mins

Translation:
Loving Mother of the Redeemer,
Who remains the open gate of heaven and the star of the sea,
Help your fallen people who strive to rise again.
You who bore the wonderment of nature,

Your holy creator,
Virgin before and after,
Receiving that 'Ave' from Gabriel,
Have mercy on us sinners. Amen.

© Oxford University Press 2021. Photocopying this copyright material is ILLEGAL.

Josquin des Prez: Alma Redemptoris Mater

78 Josquin des Prez: Alma Redemptoris Mater

Josquin des Prez: Alma Redemptoris Mater

80 Josquin des Prez: Alma Redemptoris Mater

Josquin des Prez: Alma Redemptoris Mater

82 Josquin des Prez: Alma Redemptoris Mater

Josquin des Prez: Alma Redemptoris Mater

84 Josquin des Prez: Alma Redemptoris Mater

Josquin des Prez: Alma Redemptoris Mater

86 Josquin des Prez: Alma Redemptoris Mater

17. Adoramus te, Christe

Antiphon at Feasts of the Holy Cross

ORLANDE de LASSUS
(1532–94)

Translation:
We adore you, O Christ, and we bless you,
For by your holy cross you have redeemed the world.
Lord, have mercy on us.

© Oxford University Press 2021. Photocopying this copyright material is ILLEGAL.

88 Lassus: Adoramus te, Christe

Lassus: Adoramus te, Christe

18. Adoramus te, Christe

Antiphon at Feasts of the Holy Cross

ORLANDE de LASSUS
(1532–94)

Duration: 1.5 mins

Translation:
We adore you, O Christ, and we bless you,
For by your holy cross you have redeemed the world.
Lord, have mercy on us.

© Oxford University Press 2021. Photocopying this copyright material is ILLEGAL.

12
[p]
- ctam cru - - - cem re - de - mi - sti mun -
- ctam cru - - - - cem re - de - mi - - sti
— san - ctam cru - cem re - de - mi - - sti mun-
16
[mf]
[mp]
- - dum. Do - mi - ne, mi - se - re - re
mun - dum. Do - mi - ne, mi - - se - re - re
- - dum. Do - mi - ne,— mi - se - re - re no -
20
[p]
no - - - bis, mi - se - re - - re no - bis.
no - bis, mi - se - re - - - re no - bis.
- - - bis.—

19. Agimus tibi gratias

Hymn of thanksgiving

ORLANDE de LASSUS
(1532–94)

Translation:
We give you thanks, O God, Almighty King, for all your blessings,
Who lives and reigns throughout all ages. Amen.

Duration: 1 min

© Oxford University Press 2021. Photocopying this copyright material is ILLEGAL.

13
-is tu - - is, qui vi - vis et re - -
-is tu - is, qui vi - - vis et re -
-is tu - - is, qui vi - vis et re -
16
-gnas per om - ni - a sae - cu - la sae - cu - lo - rum,
-gnas per om - ni - a sae - cu - la sae - cu - lo - rum,
-gnas per om - ni - a sae - cu - la sae - cu - lo - - rum,
19
[p]
per om - ni - a sae - cu - la sae - cu - lo - - rum.
[p]
per om - ni - a sae - cu - la sae - cu - lo - rum.
[p]
per om - ni - a sae - cu - la sae - cu - lo - rum.
22
[f]
A - - - men, a - men.
[f]
A - - - - - - men.
[f]
A - - - - - - men.

94

20. In pace in idipsum dormiam

Psalm 4: 9–10 (8)

ORLANDE de LASSUS
(1532–94)

Duration: 1.5 mins

Translation:
In peace, in peace itself, I will sleep and rest,
For you, O Lord, have singularly settled me in hope.

© Oxford University Press 2021. Photocopying this copyright material is ILLEGAL.

Lassus: In pace in idipsum dormiam **95**

21. Justus cor suum tradet

Ecclesiasticus 39: 6

ORLANDE de LASSUS
(1532–94)

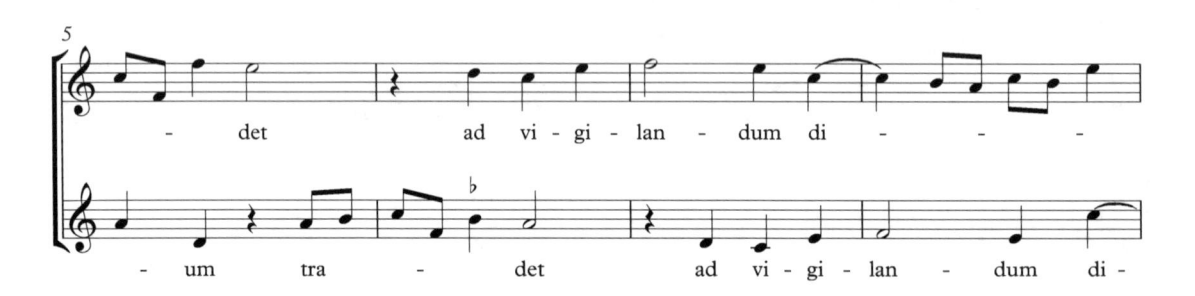

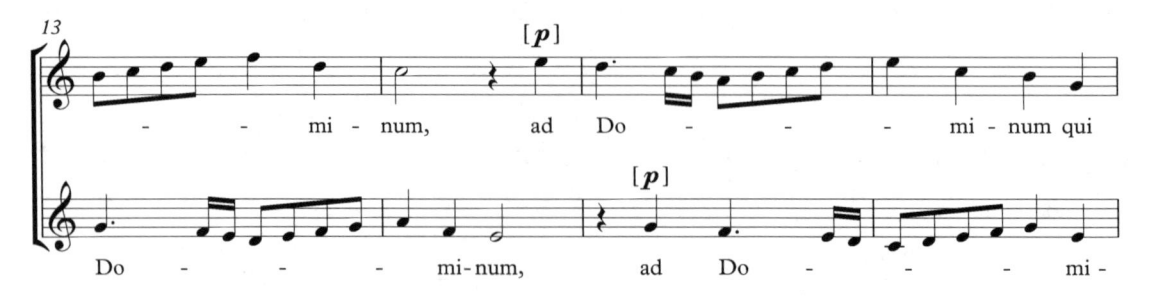

Translation:
The just man will give his heart to resort early to the Lord that made him,
And he will pray in the sight of the most High.

Duration: 1.5 mins

© Oxford University Press 2021. Photocopying this copyright material is ILLEGAL.

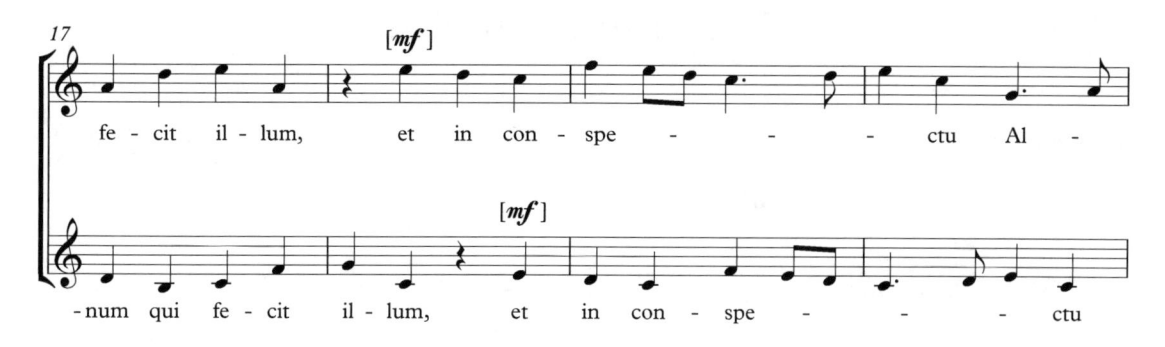

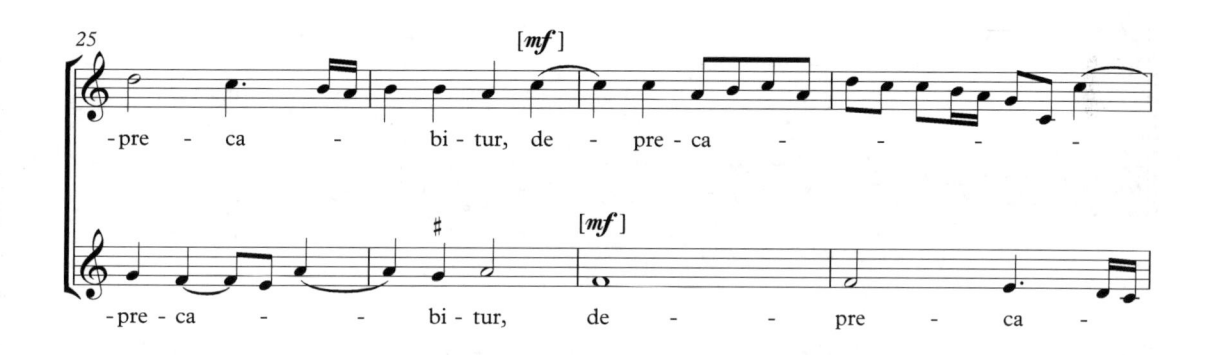

Lassus: Justus cor suum tradet

22. Oculus non vidit

1 Corinthians 2: 9

ORLANDE de LASSUS
(1532–94)

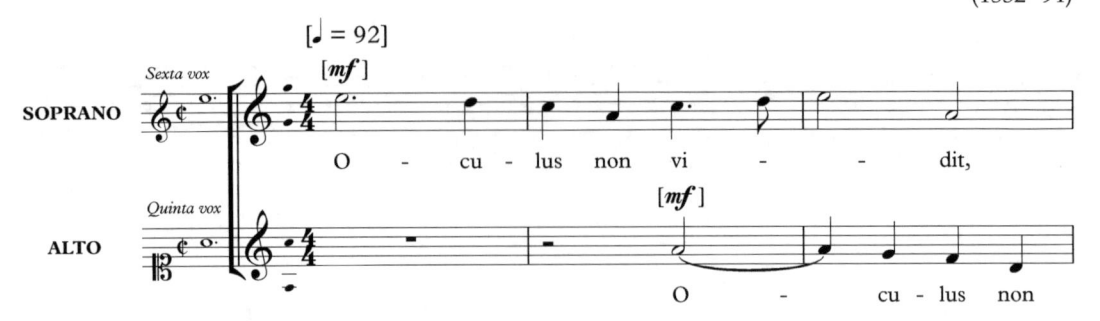

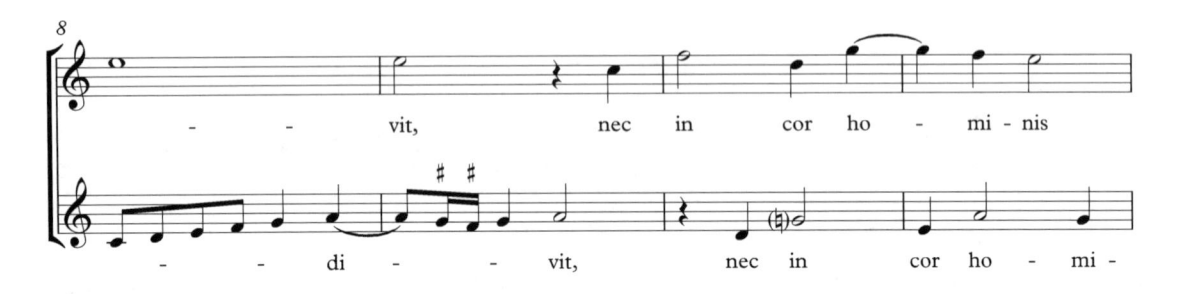

Duration: 1.5 mins

Translation:
The eye has not seen, nor the ear heard, neither have they entered into the heart of man,
What things God has prepared for those that love him.

© Oxford University Press 2021. Photocopying this copyright material is ILLEGAL.

16
quae pre - pa - ra - vit De -
quae pre - - pa - - - ra - vit De - -
20
-us his qui di - li - gunt
- us his qui di - li - gunt
24
il - - lum, qui di - li - gunt
il - - - lum, qui di - li - gunt
28
il - - - - - - - - lum.
il - - - - - - - lum.

23. Cum pervenisset beatus Andreas

Antiphon for the Feast of St Andrew

TIBURZIO MASSAINO
(*c*.1550–*c*.1608)

Duration: 3 mins

Translation:
When the blessed Andrew came to the place
Where the cross was made ready, he exclaimed and said:
O good cross, long wished for,
And now made ready for a desirous spirit,
Carefree and joyful, I come to thee,
And you gladly welcome me,
A disciple of him who once hung upon you.

© Oxford University Press 2021. Photocopying this copyright material is ILLEGAL.

Massaino: Cum pervenisset beatus Andreas

102 Massaino: Cum pervenisset beatus Andreas

29
O bo-na crux, di-u de-si-de-ra-ta,
O bo-na crux, di-u de-si-de-ra-ta, di-u de-
-na crux, O bo-na crux, di-u de-si-de-ra-ta, di-
crux, O bo-na crux, di-u de-si-de-ra-ta
O bo-na crux, di-u de-si-de-
mf

35
di-u de-si-de-ra-ta et jam con-cu-pi-
-si-de-ra-ta et jam con-
-u de-si-de-ra-ta et jam con-cu-pi-scen-ti
et jam con-cu-pi-scen-ti a-ni-mo
-ra-ta et jam con-cu-pi-scen-ti a-ni-
cresc.

104 Massaino: Cum pervenisset beatus Andreas

Massaino: Cum pervenisset beatus Andreas

106 Massaino: Cum pervenisset beatus Andreas

24. Surge, propera, amica mea

Song of Songs 2: 10b–13a

TIBURZIO MASSAINO
(c.1550–c.1608)

Duration: 3 mins

Translation:
Arise, hasten, my love, and come away.
For now the winter is past, the rain is over and gone.
The flowers appear on the earth.
The time of pruning has come,

And the voice of the turtle-dove is heard in our land.
The fig tree puts forth its figs, and the vines
   are in blossom,
They give forth fragrance.

© Oxford University Press 2021. Photocopying this copyright material is ILLEGAL.

108 Massaino: Surge, propera, amica mea

Massaino: Surge, propera, amica mea

110 Massaino: Surge, propera, amica mea

Massaino: Surge, propera, amica mea **111**

112 Massaino: Surge, propera, amica mea

Massaino: Surge, propera, amica mea

114 Massaino: Surge, propera, amica mea

Massaino: Surge, propera, amica mea **115**

116 Massaino: Surge, propera, amica mea

25. Dum illucescente

Feast of St Mark the Evangelist
Sermones, Petrus Damiani (c.1007–72)

CLAUDIO MERULO
(1533–1604)

Translation:
At the dawning of the solemnity of St Mark,
Our Easter joy is doubled.

Duration: 2 mins

© Oxford University Press 2021. Photocopying this copyright material is ILLEGAL.

118 Merulo: Dum illucescente

Merulo: Dum illucescente **119**

120 Merulo: Dum illucescente

26. Jubilate Deo

Introit for the Third Sunday after Easter
Psalm 97 (98): 4

CLAUDIO MERULO
(1533–1604)

Duration: 1 min

Translation:
O be joyful in the Lord, all ye lands:
Sing, and exult, and praise.

© Oxford University Press 2021. Photocopying this copyright material is ILLEGAL.

122 Merulo: Jubilate Deo

Merulo: Jubilate Deo

124

27. Ave Maria

The Angelic Salutation

CLAUDIO MONTEVERDI
(1567–1643)

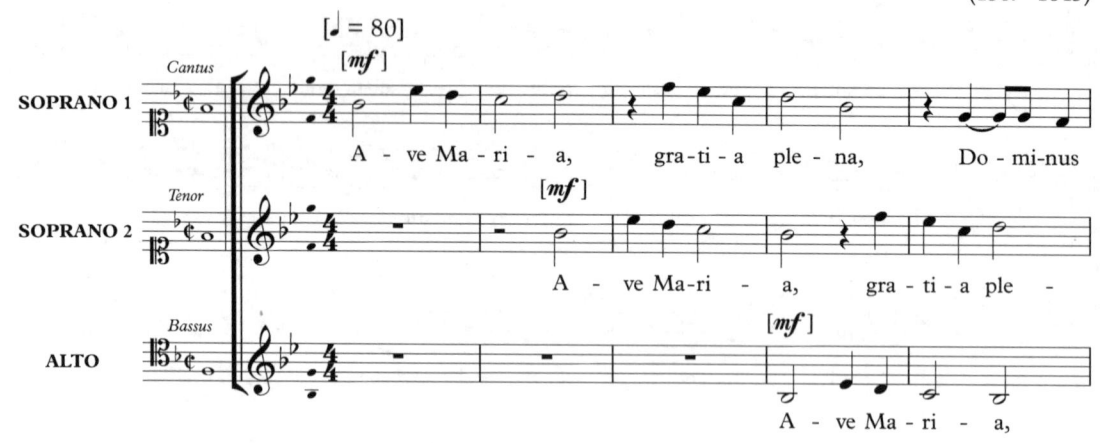

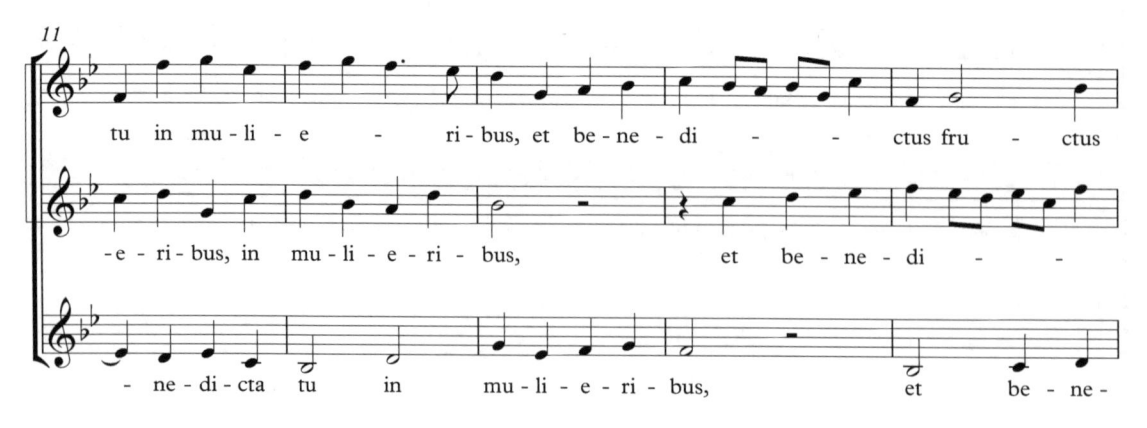

Duration: 1.5 mins

Translation:
Hail Mary, full of grace, the Lord is with thee,
Blessed art thou among women,
   and blessed is the fruit of thy womb, Jesus.

Holy Mary, Mother of God,
Pray for us sinners,
   now and at the hour of our death. Amen.

© Oxford University Press 2021. Photocopying this copyright material is ILLEGAL.

Monteverdi: Ave Maria 125

28. Lauda Sion

Sequence for the Feast of Corpus Christi
St Thomas Aquinas (1225–74)

CLAUDIO MONTEVERDI
(1567–1643)

Translation:
Sion, praise your saviour,
Praise your leader and shepherd in hymns and canticles.
Dare as much as you can,
Because he is greater than praise,
Nor can you praise him enough.

Good Shepherd, true bread,
Jesus, have mercy on us,
Feed us, protect us,
Make us see good things in the land of the living.

Duration: 1.5 mins

© Oxford University Press 2021. Photocopying this copyright material is ILLEGAL.

Monteverdi: Lauda Sion

29. O Domine Jesu Christe

Palm Sunday and Feasts of the Holy Cross
Attrib. Pope Gregory I

CLAUDIO MONTEVERDI
(1567–1643)

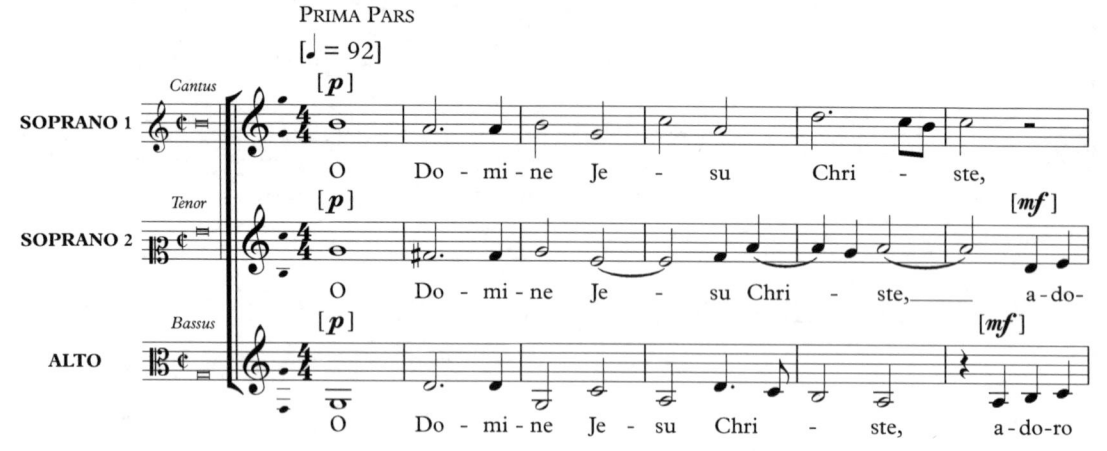

Duration: 3 mins

Translation:
O Lord Jesus Christ,
I adore thee hanging on the cross,
Wearing a crown of thorns upon thy head,
I beg thee, that thy cross may free me
 from the deceiving angel. Amen.

O Lord Jesus Christ,
I adore thee wounded on the cross,
Given gall and vinegar to drink.
I beg thee, that thy wounds may be
 the remedy of my soul. Amen.

© Oxford University Press 2021. Photocopying this copyright material is ILLEGAL.

Monteverdi: O Domine Jesu Christe

130 Monteverdi: O Domine Jesu Christe

30. O magnum mysterium

Feast of the Nativity of Our Lord

CRISTÓBAL de MORALES
(*c*.1500–53)

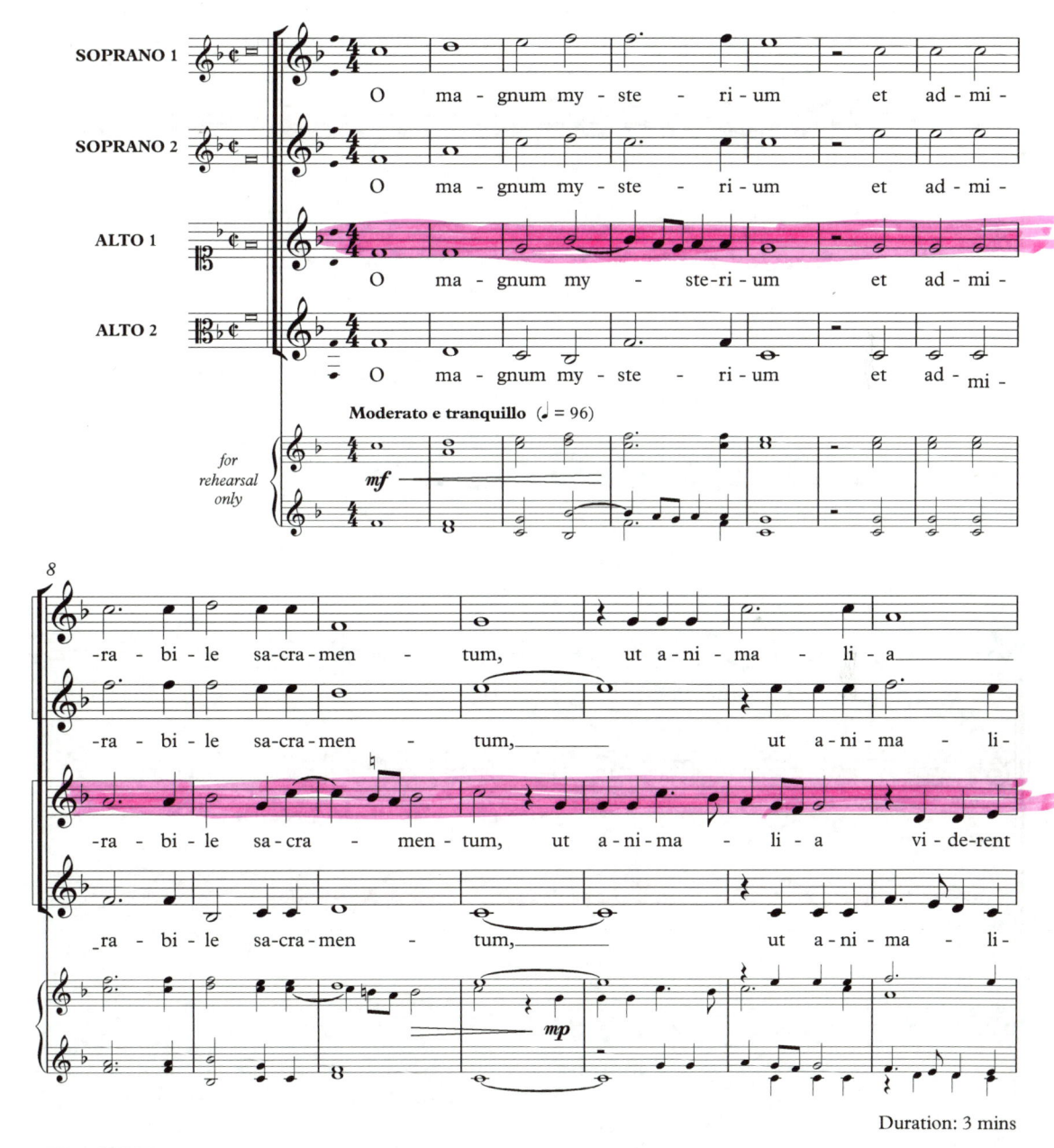

Moderato e tranquillo (♩ = 96)

Duration: 3 mins

Translation:
O great mystery and wonderful sacrament,
That animals should see the new-born Lord lying in a manger:
O blessed Virgin, whose womb was worthy to bear Christ the Lord.

Lord, I heard your voice and was afraid,
I considered your works and I trembled:
Between two animals.

132 Morales: O magnum mysterium

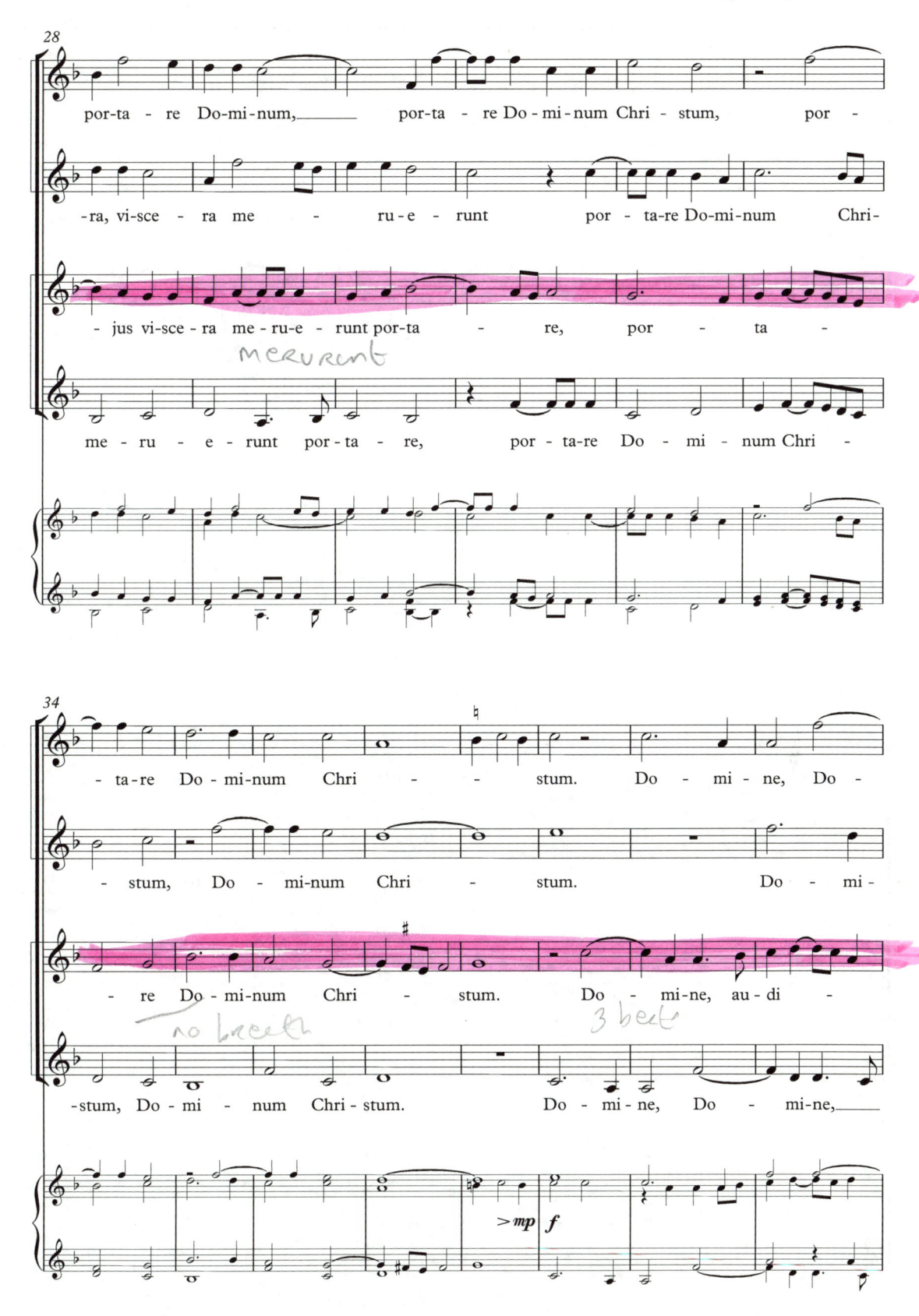

Morales: O magnum mysterium **133**

42
-mi-ne, au - di - vi, Do - mi-ne, au-di - vi au-di - tum tu -
-ne, au - - di - vi au-di - tum
-vi, Do - mi-ne, au-di-vi au-di - tum tu - um et ti -
Do - mi - ne, au-di-vi au-di - tum tu - um et ti -
48
-um et ti - mu - i: con - si-de - ra - vi o-pe - ra tu -
tu-um et ti - mu - i: con - si-de - ra - vi o - pe - ra tu -
- mu - i: con - si-de - ra - vi o-pe - ra tu - a, et
- mu - i: con - si-de - ra - vi o-pe - ra tu - a,
mf
cresc.
f

54
-a, et ex-pa - vi: in me-di-o du - o-rum a - ni-ma-li - um,
-a, et ex-pa - - - vi: in me-di-
ex - pa - - - vi: in me-di-o du - o-rum a - ni-ma - li - um, du-
4 beats
careful space
et ex-pa - - vi: in me-di - o du -
mp
cresc.
61
in me-di - o du - o - rum a - ni-ma - li - um.
-o du - o-rum a - ni- ma - li - um, a - ni - ma - li - um.
- o-rum a - ni - ma - li - um.
no breath
-o - rum a - ni - ma - li-um, a - ni-ma - li - - um.
mf

31. Regina caeli

Marian Antiphon at Eastertide

CRISTÓBAL de MORALES
(c.1500–53)

Duration: 2.5 mins

Translation:
Rejoice, Queen of Heaven, alleluia,
For he, whom thou wast worthy to bear, alleluia,
Has risen as he said, alleluia,
Pray for us to God, alleluia.

© Oxford University Press 2021. Photocopying this copyright material is ILLEGAL.

Morales: Regina caeli **137**

138 Morales: Regina caeli

35
-xit, re - sur - re - xit, si - cut di - -
- sur-re - xit, si - cut di - xit, si-cut di - xit, si-
Re - sur - re - - xit, si - cut
Re - sur-re - xit, si - cut di - xit, re - sur - re - xit, si - cut_ di -

41
- - xit, al - le - lu - - ia, al - le - lu -
- cut di - - - - xit, al - le - lu -
di - xit, al - le - lu - ia.
-xit, al - le - lu - ia, al - le - lu -

47
-ia. O-ra pro no-bis De - - - - - -
-ia. O - ra pro no-bis De - um, o - ra pro no - bis De -
O - ra pro no - bis De - um,
-ia. O - ra pro no-bis De - um, o - ra pro
mp
53
- - - um, al - le - lu - - ia,
-um, al - le - lu - ia, al - le -
o - ra pro no - bis De - um, al - le -
no-bis De - - - - - - um, al - le -
mf

Morales: Regina caeli

32. Alma Redemptoris Mater

Marian Antiphon attrib. Hermann of Reichenau (d. 1054)
First Sunday of Advent

GIOVANNI PIERLUIGI da PALESTRINA
(1525–94)

Duration: 4 mins

Translation:
Loving mother of the redeemer,
Who remains the open gate of heaven and the star of the sea,
Help your fallen people who strive to rise again.
You who bore the wonderment of nature,
Your holy creator,
Virgin before and after,
Receiving that 'Ave' from Gabriel,
Have mercy on us sinners.

© Oxford University Press 2021. Photocopying this copyright material is ILLEGAL.

Palestrina: Alma Redemptoris Mater **143**

144 Palestrina: Alma Redemptoris Mater

38
sur - ge - re, sur - ge - re qui
- ti, sur - ge - re, sur - ge - re
- ti, sur - ge - re, sur - ge - re qui cu - rat
- ti, sur - ge - re, sur - ge - re qui cu - rat po - pu-
mp mf
44
cu - rat po - pu - lo, qui cu - rat,
qui cu - rat po - pu - lo,
po-pu - lo, qui cu-rat po - pu - lo, qui cu - rat po - pu - lo,
- lo, qui cu - rat po-pu - lo, qui cu - rat

146 Palestrina: Alma Redemptoris Mater

Palestrina: Alma Redemptoris Mater

148 Palestrina: Alma Redemptoris Mater

Palestrina: Alma Redemptoris Mater

150 Palestrina: Alma Redemptoris Mater

33. Confitemini Domino

Tract on 2nd Sunday of Lent
Psalm 117 (118): 1

GIOVANNI PIERLUIGI da PALESTRINA
(1525–94)

Translation:
O give thanks to the Lord, for he is gracious, for his mercy endures forever.

Duration: 1.5 mins

© Oxford University Press 2021. Photocopying this copyright material is ILLEGAL.

11
- ni-am bo - nus, quo - ni-am bo - - - -
-no, quo - ni-am bo - nus, quo - ni-am bo - nus, quo - ni-
-no, quo - ni-am bo - nus, quo -
-no, quo - ni - am bo-nus, quo - ni-am
16
- nus, quo-ni-am in sae - - cu - lum mi-se-ri-
-am bo - nus, quo - ni-am in sae-cu-lum mi - se-ri-cor-di-
-ni-am bo - nus, quo-ni-am in sae-cu - lum mi-se-ri - cor-di-a e-
bo - nus, quo-ni-am in sae - - cu - lum
mf
mp

Palestrina: Confitemini Domino

154 Palestrina: Confitemini Domino

34. Jesu, Rex admirabilis

Office Hymn for the Feast of the Holy Name
attrib. St Bernard of Clairvaux (1090–1153)

GIOVANNI PIERLUIGI da PALESTRINA
(1525–94)

Translation:
Jesus, wondrous king and noble conqueror,
Ineffable delight, wholly to be desired.

Remain with us, O Lord, and shine your light upon us,
Dispel the darkness of our minds and fill the world with your sweetness. Amen.

Duration: 1.5 mins

© Oxford University Press 2021. Photocopying this copyright material is ILLEGAL.

156

35. Pueri Hebraeorum

Antiphon for Palm Sunday

GIOVANNI PIERLUIGI da PALESTRINA
(1525–94)

Duration: 2 mins

Translation:
The Hebrew children, bearing olive branches, went forth to meet the Lord,
Crying out and saying: Hosanna in the highest.

© Oxford University Press 2021. Photocopying this copyright material is ILLEGAL.

Palestrina: Pueri Hebraeorum

158 Palestrina: Pueri Hebraeorum

Palestrina: Pueri Hebraeorum

160 Palestrina: Pueri Hebraeorum

36. Magnificat

Canticle of the BVM
Luke 1: 46–55

JOHN SHEPPARD
(*c*.1515–58)

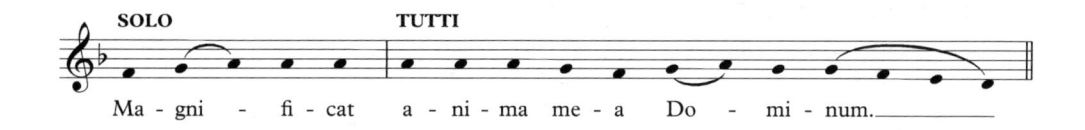

Duration: 10 mins

Translation:
My soul doth magnify the Lord.
And my spirit hath rejoiced in God my Saviour.
For he hath regarded the lowliness of his handmaiden.
For behold from henceforth all generations shall call me blessed.
For he that is mighty hath magnified me, and holy is his Name.
And his mercy is on them that fear him, throughout all generations.
He hath shewed strength with his arm,
   he hath scattered the proud in the imagination of their hearts.
He hath put down the mighty from their seat,
   and hath exalted the humble and meek.

He hath filled the hungry with good things,
   and the rich he hath sent empty away.
He remembering his mercy hath holpen his
   servant Israel,
As he promised to our forefathers,
   Abraham and his seed for ever.
Glory be to the Father, and to the Son,
   and to the Holy Ghost,
As it was in the beginning, is now,
   and ever shall be, world without end. Amen.

© Oxford University Press 2021. Photocopying this copyright material is ILLEGAL.

8
-ri-tus me - - - - - - - - - us in De -
-vit spi - ri-tus me - - - - - - - us in
- us, spi - ri-tus me - - - - us in De - - -
- - - - - - - - - - - - - us in De -
mf
13
- - - - - - - - - - o sa - lu - ta - ri me -
De - - - - - - - - - o sa - lu - ta - ri me -
- - - - - - - - - - o sa - lu - ta - ri me -
- - - - - - - - - - o sa - lu - ta - ri me -

Sheppard: Magnificat

164 Sheppard: Magnificat

45
et san-ctum no - men e - - - - - -
est, et san-ctum no - men e -
no - men e - - - - - - - - jus, et
et san-ctum no - men e - - - - - - - - -
51
-jus, et san-ctum no - men e - - - - - - - - -
- - - - - - - jus, et san-ctum no - men e - -
san-ctum no - men e - - - jus, et san-ctum no - men e -
- jus, et san-ctum

166 Sheppard: Magnificat

74
su - - - - o,
- - - - - - o, di - sper - sit su -
- - - - - - o, di - sper - sit su - per -
- - - - - - o,
mp f
82
men - te
- per - - - - - - - - bos men -
- - - - - - - - - bos men -
di - sper - sit su - per - - bos men - te

168 Sheppard: Magnificat

cor - dis su - i, men - te cor - dis

-te cor - dis su - i, men - te cor - dis su -

-te cor - dis su - i, men - te cor - dis su -

cor - dis su - i, men - te cor - dis su -

su - i, men - te cor - dis su -

— — — — — — i, men - te cor -

— i, men - te cor - dis su - — cor -

— — i, men - te cor - dis su -

Sheppard: Magnificat

120
-ri - en - - - - tes im -
- - - - tes im - ple-vit bo - - - - - -
- - - - tes im - ple-vit bo - - - - - -
-su - ri - en - - - tes im - ple - vit bo -
cresc.
126
-ple-vit bo - - - - - - - - - - -
- - nis, im - ple-vit bo - - - - - - -
-nis, im-ple-vit bo - - - - - - - - - -
- - nis, im-ple-vit bo - - - - - -

132
-nis, et di - vi - - - - - - - - -
-nis,
- nis, di - mi -
- nis, et di - vi - - - - - - - -
mp
138
- - - - - - - tes di - mi - sit in - a - -
di - mi - sit in - a - - - - - - nes, di-
-sit in - a - - - - - nes, di - mi - sit in - a -
- - tes di - mi - sit in - a - - - -

172 Sheppard: Magnificat

157
- - - cut lo - cu - tus est ad pa - tres no -
- - cut lo-cu-tus est ad pa - tres no - - stros, ad pa-tres
lo-cu - tus est ad pa-tres no - -
163
- - - - - - stros, A - bra-
no - - - - - - stros, A - bra - ham et se - mi -
A - bra - ham et se - mi - -
- - - - - stros, A - bra-
mp mf

168
-ham et se - mi - ni e - jus in sae - cu - - - - -
- - - - - - - ni e - jus in
- - - ni e - jus in sae - cu - - - - -
-ham et se - mi - - ni e - jus in sae - cu -
173
- la, e - jus in sae - cu - - - - - la.
sae - cu - - - - - - - - la.
-la, e - jus in sae - cu - - - la, e - jus in sae - cu - la.
- - - - - - - - - - - la.
p
179
Glo - ri - - a Pa - tri, et Fi - li - o,
180
et Spi - ri - tu - i San - cto.

181
Si - - - - - - - - - - - -
Si - - - - - - - - -
Si - - - - - - - - - - - -
Si - cut
f
187
- - - - - - cut e - rat in prin - ci - pi - -
- - - - - - - - - - cut e - rat in prin - ci -
- - - - cut e - rat in prin - ci - pi - -
e - - rat in prin - ci - pi - o,

176 Sheppard: Magnificat

205
- - - la sae - cu-lo-rum. A - - - - - men, sae - cu -
-la sae-cu-lo-rum. A - - - - men, sae-cu-lo-rum, a -
- - - - - la sae-cu-lo-rum. A - - - - -
- la sae - cu-lo-rum. A - - - men, sae - cu - lo - rum, a -
211
-lo-rum, a - - - - - - - - - - men.
- - - - - - - - - - men.
- men, sae - cu - lo-rum, a - - - - - - - - men.
- - - - - - - - - - - men.

37. Audivi vocem de caelo

Responsory for the Feast of All Saints
(Jeremiah 40: 10; Matthew 25: 6)

JOHN TAVERNER
(c.1490–1545)

Duration: 3 mins

Translation:
I heard a voice coming from heaven: come, all wisest virgins.
Fill your vessels with oil for the bridegroom is coming.
In the middle of the night there was a cry; behold, the bridegroom comes.

© Oxford University Press 2021. Photocopying this copyright material is ILLEGAL.

Taverner: Audivi vocem de caelo

180 Taverner: Audivi vocem de caelo

Taverner: Audivi vocem de caelo

40
- - - sus ve - - - - - - - -
- - - sus ve - - - - -
- sus ve - - - - - - - - - -
44
ve - - - - - - nit.
- - - - - - - - - - - - - nit.
- - - - - - - - - - - - nit.
- - - - - - - - - - - - nit.
dim.
p
48
[SEMI-CHORUS]
O - le - um re - con - di - te in va - - - sis ve - stris
49
dum spon - - sus ad - ve - ne - - rit.

38. Duo Seraphim

Matins responsory for Trinity Sunday
(Isaiah 6: 3)

TOMÁS LUIS de VICTORIA
(1548–1611)

Duration: 3 mins

Translation:
Two seraphim cried to one another:
Holy, holy, holy is the Lord, God of hosts,
All the earth is full of his glory.

There are three that bear witness in heaven,
  the Father, the Word, and the Holy Spirit;
And these three are one.

© Oxford University Press 2021. Photocopying this copyright material is ILLEGAL.

184 Victoria: Duo Seraphim

20
-oth, Do - mi-nus De - us Sa - - - ba - oth.
- mi-nus De - us Sa - - ba - oth. Ple - na est,
-oth, Do - mi-nus De - us Sa - ba - oth. Ple-
-oth, Do - mi-nus De - us Sa - ba - oth, Sa - ba - oth.
25
Ple - na est om - nis ter - ra glo-ri-a e -
ple - na est om - nis ter - ra glo - ri - a
- na est, ple - na est om - nis ter - ra glo - ri - a
Ple - na est om - nis ter - ra glo-ri-a e -
f

186 Victoria: Duo Seraphim

Victoria: Duo Seraphim **187**

188 Victoria: Duo Seraphim

Victoria: Duo Seraphim

190 Victoria:Duo Seraphim

39. Judas mercator pessimus

Responsory at 2nd Nocturn for Maundy Thursday

TOMÁS LUIS de VICTORIA
(1548–1611)

Translation:

Judas, the worst merchant,
Required a kiss from the Lord,
And he, like an innocent lamb,
Did not reject the kiss of Judas.
For a number of coins, he delivered Christ to the Jews.
It would have been better for him if he had never been born.

Duration: 2.5 mins

© Oxford University Press 2021. Photocopying this copyright material is ILLEGAL.

192 Victoria: Judas mercator pessimus

Victoria: Judas mercator pessimus

194 Victoria: Judas mercator pessimus

40. O Regem caeli

Feast of the Nativity of Our Lord

TOMÁS LUIS de VICTORIA
(1548–1611)

Translation:
O King of heaven, whom such great homage serves,
He is laid in a stable who holds the world,
He lies in the manger and reigns in heaven. Alleluia.

Today a Saviour is born for us, who is Christ the Lord,
in the city of David.
He lies in the manger and reigns in heaven. Alleluia.

© Oxford University Press 2021. Photocopying this copyright material is ILLEGAL.

196 Victoria: O Regem caeli

Victoria: O Regem caeli

198 Victoria: O Regem caeli

Victoria: O Regem caeli

200 Victoria: O Regem caeli

Victoria: O Regem caeli **201**

202 Victoria: O Regem caeli

Victoria: O Regem caeli

204 Victoria: O Regem caeli

105
-le - lu - ia, al - le - lu - ia, al -
-le - lu - ia, al - le - lu - ia, al - le - lu - ia, al -
Al - le - lu - ia, al - le - lu - ia, al -
-le - lu - ia, al - le - lu - ia, al -
mp
f
111
-le - lu - ia, al - le - lu - ia, al - le -
-le - lu - ia, al - le - lu - ia, al - le -
-le - lu - ia, al - le - lu - ia, al - le - lu - ia,
-le - lu - ia, al - le - lu - ia, al - le - lu -

116
- lu - ia, al - le - lu - ia, al - le -
-lu - - ia, al - le - lu - ia, al - le - - - - lu -
al - le - - - lu - ia, al - le - lu - -
-ia, al - le - lu - ia, al - le - lu - - ia, al -
cresc.

121
-lu - ia, al - le - lu - - - ia.
-ia, al - le - lu - ia, al - le - lu - ia.
-ia, al - le - lu - ia.
- le - lu - - ia, al - le - lu - ia.

41. O sacrum convivium

Antiphon for the Feast of Corpus Christi

TOMÁS LUIS de VICTORIA
(1548–1611)

Duration: 3.5 mins

Translation:
O sacred banquet, in which Christ is received,
The memory of his Passion is recalled.
The mind is filled with grace,
And a pledge of future glory is given to us. Alleluia.

© Oxford University Press 2021. Photocopying this copyright material is ILLEGAL.

208 Victoria: O sacrum convivium

23
-mo - ri-a, me - mo - - ri - a
-tur me - mo - - - - ri - a pas - si - o - nis e - -
-co - li - tur me - mo - ri - a pas - si - o - nis e - -
-tur me - mo - - - ri - a pas - si - o - nis e - -
mp p cresc.

29
pas - si - o - nis e - - - - - - jus.
-jus, pas - si - o - - nis e - - - - jus.
-jus, pas - si - o - nis e - - - - - jus.
-jus, pas - si - o - - nis e - - - - jus.
p mf
p

210 Victoria: O sacrum convivium

SECUNDA PARS

Victoria: O sacrum convivium **211**

212 Victoria: O sacrum convivium

Victoria: O sacrum convivium

42. O vos omnes

Responsory at 2nd Nocturn for Holy Saturday
Lamentations 1: 12

TOMÁS LUIS de VICTORIA
(1548–1611)

Duration: 2.5 mins

Translation:
O all of you that pass this way, attend and see
If there be any sorrow like my sorrow.
Attend, all you people, and see my sorrow.

13
et vi - de - te, Si est
-de - - - - te, Si est do - lor
- - - - te, Si est do - lor si -
-de - - - - te, Si est do - lor
p cresc.
mf
19
FINE
do - lor si - mi - lis si - cut do - lor me - us.
si - - - mi - lis si - cut do - lor me - us.
- mi - lis, si - mi - lis si - cut do - lor me - us.
si - - - mi - lis si - cut do - lor me - us.
FINE
mp
pp

216 Victoria: O vos omnes

43. Tenebrae factae sunt

Responsory at 2nd Nocturn for Good Friday

TOMÁS LUIS de VICTORIA
(1548–1611)

Andante espressivo (𝅘𝅥 = 72)

Duration: 4 mins

Translation:
Darkness fell when the Jews crucified Jesus,
And about the ninth hour Jesus cried out in a loud voice:
My God, why have you forsaken me?
And bowing his head, he gave up his spirit.
Jesus cried out in a loud voice and said:
Father, into your hands I commend my spirit.

© Oxford University Press 2021. Photocopying this copyright material is ILLEGAL.

218 Victoria: Tenebrae factae sunt

26
me de-re-li - qui - sti, de - re - li - qui - sti?
quid me de - re - li - qui-sti, de - re - li - qui - sti? Et in -
ut quid me de - re - li - qui - - sti? Et in - cli-
-sti, de-re-li - qui - sti, de - re - li - qui - sti? Et in -
p
pp
p

33
FINE
E - mi-sit spi - - - ri - tum.
- cli-na - to ca - pi - te e - mi-sit spi-ri - tum.
-na - to ca - pi - te e - mi-sit spi - - ri - tum.
- cli-na - to ca - pi - te e - mi-sit spi-ri - tum.
FINE
pp

220 Victoria: Tenebrae factae sunt

COMMENTARY

Notes
A shorthand system to identify the variants found in the sources is employed as follows: bar number (Arabic), voice (S1, S2, A1, A2, *etc.*), and symbol number in the bar (Roman). For example, in *Magi videntes stellam*, 11 S1 *vii* refers to bar 11, Soprano 1, last note of the bar.

1. Agazzari: *Magi videntes stellam*
Celebrated as one of the most prominent theorists of the early baroque period due to the influential publication *Del sonare sopra'l basso con tutti li stromenti e dell'uso loro nel conserto* (Siena, 1607), Agostino Agazzari spent the majority of his professional life working at Siena Cathedral. From 1604 to 1607 he held posts in Rome at the Collegio Germanico and the Seminario Romano before returning to the Tuscan 'City of the Virgin'. The Epiphany motet *Magi videntes stellam*, originally scored for three tenors, was published in Johann Donfrid's *Promptuarii musici concentus ecclesiasticos*. The skilful art of word-painting, coupled with rhythmic energy, makes this an attractive motet for Christmastide. Many of the pieces in Donfrid's collection offer alternative voicing suggestions, and while the original scoring may tentatively have represented the three wise men, the piece works equally well transposed up a ninth for upper voices.
Source: D-Mbs, *Promptuarii musici concentus ecclesiasticos* (Strasbourg, 1622).

2. Certon: *Ave Maria*
In 1536 Pierre Certon was appointed Master of the Choristers at the Sainte-Chapelle in Paris, a position he held until his death in 1572. Although he is more famous for the development of the secular chanson, his sacred output included eight mass settings, as well as psalm settings, motets, and chansons spirituelles. Throughout Certon's sacred works there is a clear influence of his predecessor at the Sainte-Chapelle, Claudin de Sermisy, while a propensity for plainchant themes dominates the thematic material. This is evident in his short three-part setting of the Marian text *Ave Maria*, where the first two phrases of the plainchant melody serve as a *cantus firmus*.
Source: GB-Lbl, *Libro secondo de li motetti a tre voce* (Venice, 1549). Also consulted: US-PHu, *Petri Certon Institutoris Symphoniacorum puerorum Sancti Sacelli Parisiensis recens modulorum editio* (Paris, 1542).

3. Cifra: *Ex ore infantium*
Antonio Cifra became *maestro di cappella* at Santa Casa, Loreto, in 1609 and his compositional output includes eight books of *concertato* motets for voices and organ, which enjoyed several reprints, as well as two volumes of mass settings. Considered one of the Roman school of church composers, along with Gregorio Allegri, Paolo Agostino, and Orazio Benevoli, Cifra's compositional style merges the traditional polyphony of Palestrina with the more contemporary *concertato* style. The popularity of this new hybrid form was far-reaching, not only in Italy, but also with the German publishing market, making Cifra an illustrious ambassador of this new Roman style. The Christmas motet *Ex ore infantium* was published by Donfrid with an organ continuo accompaniment, but the piece works equally well unaccompanied. The alternation of busy rhythmic writing with homophonic statements makes this a charming motet. The notation has been transposed up a tone.
Source: D-Mbs, *Promptuarii musici concentus ecclesiasticos* (Strasbourg, 1622). *Variants*: 7 S2 i: source erroneously gives *a*.

4. Clemens non Papa: *Ego flos campi*
Jacobus Clemens non Papa was one of the most prolific composers of sacred music from the early sixteenth century. While little is known of his early years, place of birth, or education, Clemens has long been associated with the Flemish school of polyphony and was widely published throughout Europe from the 1540s. The appendage of the sobriquet 'non Papa' has fascinated scholars for decades, with theories speculating that he may have been trying to avoid confusion with Pope Clement VII, or distinguishing himself from a priest-poet from Ypres, or even ironically referring to his drunken and promiscuous behaviour. Clemens composed two settings of the Marian text *Ego flos campi*, one scored for mixed choir of seven voices and this other, more intimate, setting for three voices. Here the voices weave beautiful counterpoint with attractive independent melodies. The motet, originally scored for low voices, has been transposed up a ninth.
Source: D-Mbs, *Premier livre ... à trois parties* (Louvain, 1560).

5. Cristo: *Audi Israel*
Born in Coimbra around 1550, Pedro de Cristo joined the Augustinian monastery of Santa Cruz in 1571. He succeeded Francisco de Santa Maria as *mestre de capela* and held the same position in its sister house São Vicente de Fóra, Lisbon. All the motets by Cristo in this anthology come from the autograph choir partbook 33 and, due to their brevity, possibly date from the early part of his career. They are thought to have been copied by the composer himself and are attributed to him on stylistic grounds. The use of high clefs and narrow vocal ranges indicates performance by equal voices. The texture of this five-part Lenten motet is relentlessly dense, but the clever use of well-shaped phrases and dynamics, informed by the text, leads to an exciting interpretation.
Source: P-Cug, autograph choir partbook 33.

6. Cristo: *Dum complerentur dies Pentecostes*
Many Renaissance composers chose to set the text *Dum complerentur dies Pentecostes*, which highlights the importance of Pentecost in the liturgical calendar. The source for

this four-part motet includes 'in dies Pentecostes' in the title, confirming its use on the Day of Pentecost. Possibly one of Cristo's earlier motets, this attractive piece demonstrates a beautiful simplicity in the individual lines, shaped by homophonic writing at each cadence. This motet also employs melismatic lines to portray 'the blowing of a violent wind' and concludes with syncopated, imitative 'alleluia's.

Source: P-Cug, autograph choir partbook 33.

7. Cristo: *Princeps gloriosissime*
The strong homophonic opening of this motet, in honour of St Michael the Archangel, the defender in battle against all things evil, makes an impactful statement, before exploring the intricate weaving of imitative polyphonic writing. The closing 'alleluia's in triple metre, resolving on a tierce de Picardie, bring the motet to a satisfactory close.

Source: P-Cug, autograph choir partbook 33.

8. Anon., attrib. d'Este: *Sicut lilium inter spinas*
Few music collections were published anonymously in the sixteenth century but, of those that were, the unattributed *Musica quinque motetta: materna lingua vocata*, from the Venetian printer Girolamo Scotto in 1543, has enjoyed much research and debate. Musicologists such as Laurie Stras postulate that the composer of this collection is Leonora d'Este, daughter of Duke Alfonso I and Lucrezia Borgia. D'Este entered the Corpus Domini Convent in Ferrara at the age of 8, and by the age of 19 had become its abbess. This convent and its community were a powerhouse of music-making. Patronage was initially given by one of the founders of the Clarissan order, St Catherine of Bologna, and subsequently by d'Este's extended family. Among the convent's collection of instruments, the chapel enjoyed a very fine organ. Although there is no definitive proof of d'Este's authorship, the fact that she was female, belonging to a noble family, and a nun, precluded her from publicly owning her compositions. The texts of the collection feature standard liturgical examples, but also meditative prayers for private devotion by the Clarissan community, which further suggests her as a possible composer for at least part of the publication. The music and style of d'Este's compositions are skilful in the art of polyphonic writing and the beautiful *Sicut lilium inter spinas*, written for five voices, is a fine example of this style. This motet, originally scored for lower voices, is presented here an octave higher.

Source: D-Ju, *Musica quinque vocum: motetta materna lingua vocata* (Venice, 1543).

9. Gombert: *Quam pulchra es*
Between 1539 and 1552 the Venetian printers Scotto and Gardano released numerous collections of Gombert's compositions, which made him one of the most influential and widely disseminated composers following the death of Josquin. Little is known of Gombert's career until 1526, when he is recorded as a singer in the chapel of the Habsburg Emperor Charles V and subsequently appointed *maître des enfants*. Unofficially regarded as the court composer, he travelled with the court to Germany, Austria, Italy, and Spain. A rich texture is used in Gombert's setting of *Quam pulchra es*, with all voices singing almost all of the time. This texture is created through refined imitative contrapuntal writing, rather than homophony, and may reflect the descriptive texts from the Song of Songs, which compare the Beloved to aspects of nature. Originally scored for lower equal voices, this piece works delightfully well transposed up a ninth.

Source: D-Mbs, *Musica quatuor vocum* (Venice, 1539).

10. Guerrero: *Sancta et immaculata virginitas*
Francisco Guerrero was born in Seville in 1528 and began his musical studies under the tutelage of his elder brother Pedro. At the age of 17 Guerrero was appointed *maestro de capilla* at Jaén Cathedral on the recommendation of Cristóbal de Morales. After three years there, Guerrero returned to Seville Cathedral to act as assistant to Pedro Fernández, succeeding him in 1554. Guerrero attained an excellent reputation as a composer throughout Europe during his lifetime and his music was published in Venice, Paris, and Leuven, as well as Seville. In the Divine Office the text is a responsory for Christmas Day, but it is also used on Marian devotional days throughout the liturgical year.

Source: B-Br, *Motecta liber secundus* (Venice, 1589). Also consulted: B-Br, *Motecta quae partim quaternis* (Venice, 1597). Variants: 23 S1, S2, A: source has 'efferant' but 'efferam' was chosen to match S3 and the *Liber Usualis*.

11. Handl: *Ante luciferum genitus*
Jacobus Handl (also known as Gallus) was born in Slovenia in 1550 and worked throughout Austria, Moravia, and Bohemia. His compositional output was prolific, including twenty mass settings, most of which were published in the 1580 collection *Selectiores quaedam missae*. From 1586 to 1591 his vast four-volume collection of 374 motets, *Opus Musicum*, was published in Prague. *Ante luciferum genitus* is the first antiphon of Lauds for the Feast of the Epiphany and culminates with cascading, descending 'alleluia's. Originally scored for lower voices, the publication includes the text *ad aequales* in the index. The motet is presented here an octave higher and is very effective for upper voices.

Source: D-Mbs, *Opus Musicum* (Prague, 1586).

12. Handl: *Haec est dies*
Although there is no evidence of Handl ever visiting Italy, the influence of the Northern Italian *spezzati* style features frequently in the composer's output, and the polychoral works of Dominique Phinot may also have informed Handl's style. The Easter motet *Haec est dies*, scored for double choir, opens with an ebullient dialogue of homophonic statements, before embarking on a dance-like section that musically portrays the celebratory joy found in the text. The notation has been transposed up an octave.

Source: D-Mbs, *Opus Musicum* (Prague, 1587).

13. Handl: *O beata Trinitas*
Similar in style to *Haec est dies*, this motet embodies symbolism of the Trinity within its structure. The three

verses surrounded by a refrain of 'O beata Trinitas' may have been deliberately chosen to represent the Trinity, as it is the only example where Handl includes a true refrain. There is a compelling resemblance between the opening phrases of this motet and Phinot's *Sancta Trinitas*, which further demonstrates the latter's influence. The notation has been transposed up an octave.

Source: D-Mbs, *Opus Musicum* (Prague, 1587).

14. Handl: *O sacrum convivium*

The harmonic beauty and expressive lines found in this motet emulate the devout text of the ever-popular Eucharistic hymn O *sacrum convivium*. Handl's treatment of the text begins with spacious vocal entries, before introducing shorter phrases in quick imitation. The motet draws to a close with descending scale-like figures of resounding 'alleluia's, which resolve on a bright tierce de Picardie.

Source: D-Mbs, *Opus Musicum* (Prague, 1587).

15. Ingegneri: *Estote fortes in bello*

This motet for six voices was published in a collection of 1591, one year before the composer's death. The publication, which represented the culmination of a significant output of sacred music printed by Gardano between 1585 and 1591, contains predominantly mixed-voice compositions, with just three scored for *voci pari*. Ingegneri, born in Verona, was a chorister at the city's cathedral and may have been taught by Jacquet de Berchem and Giovanni Brevio. Following positions held in Padua and Venice, Ingegneri became *maestro di cappella* at Cremona during the late 1570s. There he cultivated the talent before him, including Claudio Monteverdi, who acknowledged him on the title pages of his first five publications. Ingegneri's setting of *Estote fortes in bello* alternates between declamatory homophonic sections and imitative contrapuntal writing, culminating in a dance-like and joyful finale of 'alleluia' statements in triple metre.

Source: I-Mc, *Sacrae cantiones, senis vocibus decantandae, liber primus* (Venice, 1591).

16. Josquin des Prez: *Alma Redemptoris Mater*

Josquin is widely regarded as the greatest composer of the early sixteenth century, and his style is considered innovative in terms of tonality, melodic imitation, and techniques of canon. This is witnessed in the music treatises published at the end of the Renaissance, including that of Gioseffo Zarlino, who used several references to Josquin's compositions. Born in France, Josquin was a choirboy or altar boy at St Géry's, Cambrai, and was recorded as a singer in the chapel of René of Anjou in Aix-en-Provence, before joining the French court at the Sainte-Chapelle, Paris. His notable patronages included the House of Sforza, Milan, before he joined the Papal Chapel in Rome around 1489, staying until 1495. In 1504 Josquin retired to the Cathedral of Condé, where he remained until his death in 1521. The Marian motet *Alma Redemptoris Mater* is one of two settings of this text composed by Josquin and possibly one of his earlier compositions. This setting is based upon the corresponding chant and opens with a canon at the unison. The Josquin scholar Willem Elders suggests that the symbolism of the canon at the opening of the *secunda pars* represents the idea of the birth of the Creator from the mother. Originally scored for low voices, the piece has here been transposed up an octave.

Sources: GB-Lbl, *Motetti de la corona, libro tertio* (Venice, 1519); D-Mbs, *Motetti de la corona, libro tertio* (Venice, 1519); E-Bcd, *Motetti de la corona, libro tertio* (Venice, 1526).

17. Lassus: *Adoramus te, Christe a 5* and 18. Lassus: *Adoramus te, Christe a 3*

Born in the Franco-Flemish town of Mons, Lassus began his initial training as a choirboy in the service of Ferrante Gonzaga, the Duke of Mantua. Following posts in Mantua, Milan, and Naples, in 1553 Lassus became *maestro di cappella* at the Basilica of St John Lateran, Rome, before accepting an invitation in 1556 to join the Munich court of Albrecht V. After some six years there, he succeeded Ludwig Daser as *maestro di cappella* and held the appointment until his death in 1594. In 1604, two of Lassus's sons, Ferdinand and Rudolph, published the monumental collection of his compositions entitled *Magnum Opus Musicum*. Hailed as one of the greatest composers of the Renaissance, Lassus's compositional output was prolific, including over 500 motets. His setting of *Adoramus te, Christe* in three parts is both intimate and devotional in style. It is largely homophonic, with some melismatic writing, before introducing imitation in subsequent phrases. The brevity and voicing make this motet particularly suitable for use as an introduction to the art of singing polyphony. In contrast to his three-part setting, the heavy texture employed in the five-part work demonstrates a more mature Lassus. The incessant use of all voices, underpinned by harmonic integrity, is quite succinct, lasting a mere twenty-six bars.

Source: DK-Kk, *Magnum Opus Musicum* (Munich, 1604).

19. Lassus: *Agimus tibi gratias*

This three-part hymn of thanksgiving is predominantly homophonic and more reminiscent of Lassus's madrigal style. The use of short note values and syncopation brings life and energy to the piece before a conservative cadence.

Source: DK-Kk, *Magnum Opus Musicum* (Munich, 1604).

20. Lassus: *In pace in idipsum dormiam*

Taking verses from Psalm 4, this text for Compline is set with delicate simplicity and contemplative musicality throughout. To open the work, a descending triad in each of the three vocal lines is treated like a canon at the unison. Homophonic writing is used only once with the word 'singularly' (*singulariter*), perhaps reflecting a sense of being at one. The melismatic lines that follow are beautifully weaved together.

Source: DK-Kk, *Magnum Opus Musicum* (Munich, 1604).

21. Lassus: *Justus cor suum tradet*

The *Cantiones Duum Vocum* are thought to have been written as a pedagogical tool featuring twelve duos, or *bicinia*, with text and a further twelve without text for instrumentalists. The volume enjoyed nine reprints prior to 1610, including a Parisian print in 1601 in which a third voice part was added. The compositions demonstrate Lassus's personal approach to the art of counterpoint rather than a textbook study. The text *Justus cor suum tradet* is taken from Ecclesiasticus and is a Vespers antiphon for the Common of One Confessor. Compositional techniques such as word-painting and the exploration of a broad tessitura are evident in the setting of the text 'most High' (*Altissimi*). The interweaving of the melodic lines, which move in a predominantly scalic fashion, enjoys quick imitation and rhythmic interplay.

Source: D-Mbs, *Cantiones Duum Vocum* (Munich, 1577). Also consulted: DK-Kk, *Magnum Opus Musicum* (Munich, 1604).

22. Lassus: *Oculus non vidit*

In contrast to the previous motet, *Oculus non vidit* includes longer melismatic phrases that reflect the text, such as the rising melodic line over three bars on the word 'ascended' (*ascendit*). This piece employs different intervals in the vocal lines, which demonstrates the progressive techniques in melodic construction and imitation used by Lassus.

Source: D-Mbs, *Cantiones Duum Vocum* (Munich, 1577). Also consulted: DK-Kk, *Magnum Opus Musicum* (Munich, 1604).

23. Massaino: *Cum pervenisset beatus Andreas*

Born in Cremona, Massaino joined the Augustinian order at Piacenza before becoming *maestro di cappella* at the Basilica of Santa Maria del Popolo, Rome, in 1571. His varied career included posts in Modena, Lodi, Innsbruck, Salzburg, and Prague, before he returned to Piacenza and then Lodi, where Massaino is referred to as *maestro di cappella* in the early 1600s. His vocal output of both sacred and secular composition is considerable, and he published many books during his lifetime. The five-part motet *Cum pervenisset beatus Andreas* is almost unique in the *voci pari* repertoire, with notation presented using five treble clefs. This motet may have been commissioned by Suor Eugenia de' Navi, Vicaress of the Augustinian house of Santa Trinità, Como, to whom Massaino dedicated his second book for five voices.

Source: D-Mbs, *Motectorum quinque vocibus, liber quartus* (Venice, 1599). Variants: 37–9: 'jam' was spelt 'iam' in the source.

24. Massaino: *Surge, propera, amica mea*

The opening of this motet displays Massaino's skill in the art of word-painting with soaring lines that play on the word 'arise' (*Surge*). Punctuated with occasional homophonic writing, the beautiful melodic lines find clever use of imitation across all voices. The *secunda pars* increases the quick imitation of the vocal lines, mirroring the excitement of the text 'the time of pruning has come' (*Tempus putationis advenit*). This, coupled with the introduction of shorter note values, creates a joyful celebration of the text from the Song of Songs.

Source: D-Mbs, *Motectorum quinque vocibus, liber quartus* (Venice, 1599).

25. Merulo: *Dum illucescente*

Born in Correggio in 1533, Merulo was appointed organist at Brescia Cathedral in 1556, and the following year became one of the organists at St Mark's Basilica, Venice. He held this position for twenty-seven years before resigning in 1584 to enter the service of the Duke of Mantua. In that same year, Merulo published a complete collection of *voci pari* motets. His setting of *Dum illucescente*, a text for the Feast of St Mark the Evangelist, is scored with high clefs. The motet is framed by two polyphonic sections that incorporate some melismatic vocal lines, while the homophonic middle section in triple time is perhaps reminiscent of Merulo's madrigal style. The notation has been transposed up a tone.

Source: F-Pn, *Il primo libro de mottetti a quattro voci pari* (Venice, 1584). Also consulted: F-Pa, *Il primo libro de mottetti a quattro voci pari* (Venice, 1584).

26. Merulo: *Jubilate Deo*

This joyous motet for Eastertide is also found in the 1584 collection of *voci pari* motets. The polyphonic writing includes both rhythmic and melismatic passages to reflect this celebratory text and concludes with a brief section in triple metre. The piece is presented here an octave higher.

Source: F-Pn, *Il primo libro de mottetti a quattro voci pari* (Venice, 1584). Also consulted: F-Pa, *Il primo libro de mottetti a quattro voci pari* (Venice, 1584).

27. Monteverdi: *Ave Maria*

Claudio Monteverdi was born in Cremona in 1567. While there are no records to substantiate Monteverdi as a choirboy in Cremona Cathedral, he acknowledges in his publications that he was a student of Marc'Antonio Ingegneri, who was *maestro di cappella* there at the time. The young Monteverdi was only 15 years old when his first collection, *Sacrae cantiunculae*, was published in 1582 by the prestigious printer Gardano in Venice. The volume contains twenty-three compositions in partbooks labelled cantus, tenor, and bass. The vocal ranges of the Marian motet *Ave Maria* are best suited to two sopranos, due to the frequent crossing of the two upper parts, and an alto. The notation has been transposed up a fourth.

Source: I-CARc, *Sacrae cantiunculae tribus vocibus* (Venice, 1582).

28. Monteverdi: *Lauda Sion*

The text *Lauda Sion*, written by St Thomas Aquinas, is the sequence for the Feast of Corpus Christi. Monteverdi set stanzas one, two, and twenty-three of the sequence, which contains twenty-four verses in total. The vocal ranges are similar to those in his setting of the *Ave Maria*, with arching vocal lines imitating at the unison before an exciting triple-metre section for the third stanza. The notation has been transposed up a fourth.

Source: I-CARc, *Sacrae cantiunculae tribus vocibus* (Venice, 1582).

29. Monteverdi: *O Domine Jesu Christe*
This motet in two parts is devotional in character, with each section opening with homophonic writing before elaborating on close imitative polyphonic lines. The motet demonstrates a mature writing style that would be expected of a composer years beyond the age of the young Monteverdi. The text is based on the first two stanzas of a prayer attributed to Pope Gregory I that contemplates the Passion of Our Lord.
Source: I-CARc, *Sacrae cantiunculae tribus vocibus* (Venice, 1582).

30. Morales: *O magnum mysterium*
Cristóbal de Morales, born in Seville in *c*.1500, is widely considered one of the most important Spanish composers of the early sixteenth century. His unique style combines Spanish expressive qualities with the stricter style of Roman polyphony, influenced by his time singing with the papal choir in Rome. The motet *O magnum mysterium* is not found in any of Morales's published works, but in three separate manuscripts in Valladolid, Madrid, and Toledo, which would indicate a certain popularity of this Christmas work. All the sources are notated with high clefs, suggesting performance by upper voices. The text set by Morales is a unique composite based on the Matins responsory for Christmas Day and the Feast of the Circumcision, differing from other settings in the final stanza and with the omission of a final 'alleluia'.
Source: E-Vp, Manuscript (Valladolid).

31. Morales: *Regina caeli*
This Marian text for Eastertide, *Regina caeli*, was set four times by Morales. This setting for four voices was first published in his 1543 collection and notated in high clefs. The simple-tone plainchant hymn is strongly referenced in each of the vocal lines, with Alto 1 dedicated as a *cantus firmus* for the majority of the piece.
Source: D-Mbs, *Moralis Hispani et multorum* (Venice, 1543).

32. Palestrina: *Alma Redemptoris Mater*
Born in 1525, Palestrina takes his name from the town in which he was born. He trained as a choirboy in the Basilica di Santa Maria Maggiore in Rome and was appointed *maestro* of the Cappella Giulia, the choir of St Peter's Basilica in the Vatican, in 1551. Following posts in the papal basilicas of St John Lateran and Santa Maria Maggiore, he returned to St Peter's in 1571 and remained in the post of *maestro* until his death in 1594. Palestrina's published collection *Motettorum quatuor vocibus* was evidently very popular, and it enjoyed several reprints in the late 1500s. It contained twenty-one motets, the majority of these scored for mixed voices, with seven notated for equal voices. The Marian motet *Alma Redemptoris Mater* seamlessly interweaves each of the four independent voices based on the solemn tone of the corresponding chant. The notation has been transposed up a minor third.
Sources: I-Md, *Motettorum quatuor vocibus ... liber secundus* (Milan, 1584); I-TVd, *Motettorum quatuor vocibus ... liber secundus* (Venice, 1596); I-Af, *Motectorum quatuor vocibus liber secundus* (Venice, 1604).

33. Palestrina: *Confitemini Domino*
This joyful motet begins with a compelling homophonic opening, before exploring imitative writing between all voices. A contrasting motif of descending scales is introduced halfway through to reflect a penitential theme of mercy.
Sources: I-Md, *Motettorum quatuor vocibus ... liber secundus* (Milan, 1584); I-TVd, *Motettorum quatuor vocibus ... liber secundus* (Venice, 1596); I-Af, *Motectorum quatuor vocibus liber secundus* (Venice, 1604).

34. Palestrina: *Jesu, Rex admirabilis*
The 1586 collection of twenty-one strophic hymns entitled *Diletto Spirituale* was undoubtedly envisaged for domestic devotional practice or private recreational use rather than for performance within the liturgy, owing to the optional accompanying tablatures for lute and keyboard. The motet *Jesu, Rex admirabilis* is largely homophonic, with only one phrase incorporating imitation. Its simplicity, however, makes it a useful Eucharistic motet in contemporary liturgy. It has been transposed up a tone.
Sources: D-Mbs, *Diletto Spirituale, Canzonette a tre et a quattro voci* (Rome, 1586); GB-Lbl, *Diletto Spirituale, Canzonette a tre et a quattro voci* (Rome, 1586).

35. Palestrina: *Pueri Hebraeorum*
Palestrina's setting of *Pueri Hebraeorum* is labelled *paribus vocibus* in the source. The text is taken from the Palm Sunday antiphon, which celebrates the entry of Jesus into Jerusalem. The calls of imitation presented at the beginning emulate the calls of the Hebrew children, before a brief homophonic phrase. The repeated 'hosanna' phrases at the end of the motet bear witness to Palestrina's mastery in contrapuntal writing. The notation has been transposed up a minor third.
Sources: I-Md, *Motettorum quatuor vocibus ... liber secundus* (Milan, 1584); I-TVd, *Motettorum quatuor vocibus ... liber secundus* (Venice, 1596); I-Af, *Motectorum quatuor vocibus liber secundus* (Venice, 1604).

36. Sheppard: *Magnificat*
John Sheppard was appointed *Informator choristarum* at Magdalen College, Oxford, in 1543 and held the position for five years before becoming a Gentleman of the Chapel Royal. The majority of his compositions are found only in the Gyffard partbooks, copied by Roger Gyffard, a fellow of Magdalen College, and the Baldwin partbooks, copied by John Baldwin. These are important sources of Tudor sacred music, as there are few concordances of the works contained in both. Sheppard's *Magnificat* for four voices is found only in the Gyffard partbooks. Possibly copied in the 1570s, this setting of the *Magnificat* is mature in style and probably dates from the reign of Queen Mary. Sometimes referred to as *Magnificat primi toni*, its structure uses the *alternatim* technique, rotating choral sections with the Tone I chant. The chant provided here is the simple tone although choirs more proficient in chant may wish to use the solemn tone or the Sarum chant. The notation has

been transposed up an octave.

Source: GB-Lbl, Gyffard partbooks, MS 17802–17805. *Variants*: 42 S1 i: ♯ found in the source has been removed to maintain harmonic integrity; 98 S2 i: ♯ found in the source has been omitted.

37. Taverner: *Audivi vocem de caelo*

Taverner's early biographical detail remains unknown until 1524, when he was a lay clerk at Tattershall Collegiate Church in Lincolnshire. Two years later he took up a post at Cardinal College (Christ Church), Oxford, where the new foundation provided a large chapel choir comprising twelve lay clerks and sixteen choristers. It is during this decade that the majority of his compositional output is thought to have been written. The influence of Robert Fayrfax is clearly evident in the choral writing throughout *Audivi vocem de caelo*, where long melismatic lines on one syllable navigate to a cadence. Taverner's choice of an upper-voice scoring for this motet may come from a tradition of five boys singing the responsory at Matins for All Saints' Day, personifying the five virgins mentioned in the lesson.

Source: GB-Lbl, Gyffard partbooks, MS 17802–17805. *Variants*: 44 S1 i: ♯ found in the source has been removed to maintain harmonic integrity.

38. Victoria: *Duo Seraphim*

The Spanish composer Tomás Luis de Victoria was born in 1548 in Ávila. He was a choirboy at Ávila Cathedral under Gerónimo de Espinar and moved to Rome in 1565 to enter training for the priesthood at the Jesuit Collegio Germanico. The motet *Duo Seraphim* is one of four compositions for equal voices, which are labelled *cum paribus vocibus* and are divided into two *partes* or sections. This motet is designated 'In Festo Trinitatis' and the compositional style demonstrates word-painting and madrigal-like features. The piece opens with a duet that may reflect the word 'Duo' in the title, and the use of three voices at the start of the *secunda pars*, coupled with the use of triple metre, may be symbolic of the Trinity. The notation has been transposed up a minor third.

Source: E-TZ, *Motecta que partim quaternis ... et alia qua plurima adiuncta* (Rome, 1583).

39. Victoria: *Judas mercator pessimus*

Victoria published his Tenebrae responsories as part of his *Officium Hebdomadae Sanctae* (Office for Holy Week) in 1585. A second and earlier source, which was completed prior to its publication, exists in manuscript at the Vatican. The Tenebrae services combined the offices of Matins and Lauds in Holy Week, which from the Middle Ages was celebrated the previous evening when daylight was fading. The responsory *Judas mercator pessimus*, listed for Maundy Thursday, would therefore have been sung at Tenebrae on Spy Wednesday. The form of the responsory is ABCB, allowing three soloists to sing the versicle section C before a tutti reprise of the B section. Victoria opens this motet with a dramatic homophonic account of Judas's betrayal of Jesus, similar to the opening of another of his responsory settings, *Jesum tradidit impius*, before a contrasting section of lyrical vocal lines presented in an imitative style.

Source: GB-Lbl, *Officium Hebdomadae Sanctae* (Rome, 1585).

40. Victoria: *O Regem caeli*

Consisting of two sections, this large-scale Christmas motet opens with a rich homophonic texture that is synonymous with Victoria's compositions. This is followed by imitation in the vocal lines before a triple-metre section of resounding 'alleluia's. The *secunda pars* begins with new melodic lines that are beautifully explored before a reprise of the music from the *prima pars*.

Source: D-MÜs, *Motecta que partim quaternis ... octonis vocibus concinuntor* (Venice, 1572).

41. Victoria: *O sacrum convivium*

Of the two settings Victoria composed with this text for the Feast of Corpus Christi, his four-part setting for upper voices comprises two sections. The sustained homophonic opening creates an ethereal sound-world, mirroring the reverence of the text of this Eucharistic hymn. The exquisite vocal lines that follow create simple but effective polyphonic writing where the sentiment of each line is crafted into each phrase. The motet concludes with declamatory 'alleluia's. The music has been transposed up a minor third.

Source: D-MÜs, *Motecta que partim quaternis ... octonis vocibus concinuntor* (Venice, 1572).

42. Victoria: *O vos omnes*

A sombre mood prevails in this responsory. Victoria captures the sorrow of the Passion by sustained homophonic writing from the start and subtle points of imitation. The form of the piece follows the traditional ABCB format. The use of a descending melodic line depicting the sorrow of the text is one example of Victoria's subtle use of word-painting found in these responsories.

Source: GB-Lbl, *Officium Hebdomadae Sanctae* (Rome, 1585).

43. Victoria: *Tenebrae factae sunt*

The darkness evoked in this piece mirrors not only the title word 'Tenebrae', but also the intense grief of the crucifixion, as Jesus gives up his spirit. Although a tradition exists where this responsory can be performed an octave lower by male voices, such practice was not prescriptive by the composer and probably only dates from the eighteenth century.

Source: GB-Lbl, *Officium Hebdomadae Sanctae* (Rome, 1585).